# PROPHECIES OF LEVIATHAN

# Prophecies of Leviathan

READING PAST MELVILLE

Peter Szendy

*Translated, with an Afterword, by Gil Anidjar*

*Fordham University Press*

NEW YORK ‡ 2010

Fordham University Press has no responsibility for the persistence
or accuracy of URLs for external or third-party Internet websites
referred to in this publication and does not guarantee that any
content on such websites is, or will remain, accurate or appropriate.

Library of Congress Cataloging-in-Publication Data

Szendy, Peter.
    [Prophéties du texte-Léviathan. English]
    Prophecies of Leviathan : reading past Melville / Peter Szendy ;
translated, with an afterword, by Gil Anidjar. — 1st ed.
        p.   cm.
    Includes bibliographical references.
    ISBN 978-0-8232-3153-9 (alk. paper)
    ISBN 978-0-8232-3154-6 (pbk. : alk. paper)
    1. Melville, Herman, 1819–1891. Moby Dick.   I. Title.
PS2384.M62S9813   2010
813'.3—dc22

                              2009043533

*Prophecies of Leviathan: Reading Past Melville* was originally
published in French as Peter Szendy, *Les prophéties du texte-
Léviathan: Lire selon Melville* © 2004 by Les Éditions de Minuit,
Paris.

This work has been published with the assistance of the French
Ministry of Culture—National Center for the Book.

Ouvrage publié avec le concours du Ministère français chargé de la
culture—Centre National du Livre.

Printed in the United States of America
12 11 10   5 4 3 2 1
First edition

# CONTENTS

# ABBREVIATIONS OF WORKS BY MELVILLE

WHERE NO ABBREVIATION IS GIVEN, the citation is from *Moby-Dick, or The Whale* (Evanston, Ill: Northwestern University Press and the Newberry Library, 1988). Numbers refer to chapter and page.

ATT   "The Apple-Tree Table; or, Original Spiritual Manifestations." In *The Piazza Tales and Other Prose Pieces, 1839–1860*, 378–97. Evanston, Ill.: Northwestern University Press and the Newberry Library, 1987.

IP   *Israel Potter: His Fifty Years of Exile*. Evanston, Ill.: Northwestern University Press and the Newberry Library , 1982). Numbers refer to chapter and page.

LRM   "The Lightning-Rod Man." In *The Piazza Tales and Other Prose Pieces, 1839–1860*, 118–24. Evanston, Ill.: Northwestern University Press and the Newberry Library, 1987.

TM   "The Tartarus of Maids." In *The Piazza Tales and Other Prose Pieces, 1839–1860*, 323–35. Evanston, Ill.: Northwestern University Press and the Newberry Library, 1987.

# Reading and the Right to Death

TO READ MELVILLE—such will have been my project. Yet I very quickly found myself confronted with this evidence: to read Melville, and *Moby-Dick* in particular (it was the great novel of my childhood, when my father brought to life some of its passages for me, in his hotel room, which resembled Jonah's cabin in chapter 9), is *to read what reading means.* This is why reading Melville is an abyssal enterprise, which demands, finally, that one read reading—and thus, in a very precise sense, which I will try to indicate here, demands *re-reading.*[1]

THESE *PROPHECIES*, as I will call them for the sake of brevity (leaving out a part of my heading), end with a "scene" in which a number of heads fall: the head of Leviathan himself (the whale) whose beheading Ishmael narrates in chapter 70 of *Moby-Dick*; the head of the regal chimney in Melville's short story "I and My Chimney," which ceaselessly accompanied my reading of the great novel, all the way to its last page, where a regicidal decollation occurs; and, above all, the head of the text itself, delivered to a space in which reading is said to be "without end," "without heading," "without head." If one takes Melville at his word, a word around which *Prophecies* does not cease to turn ("Leviathan is the text"), the beheading of Leviathan is also, indissociably, the beheading of the text. Yet it is at the very instant in which it loses its head that the text sends and dispatches itself, in the open address to the other that closes *Prophecies*. "Once again, it is your turn." And if I recall this final staging here, it is in order to mark or re-mark that the high stakes of *Prophecies* were, I realize it now, about the sovereignty of the text. Which is to say, its life and its death in and through reading. If, as I have been suggesting, a text can be beheaded in the manner of a king, what then happens to it?

In a preliminary fashion (as a premise of sorts toward a book to come on the *politics of reading*), *Prophecies* can be situated in the space opened by this question. Between this book and the one in progress, I would therefore like to insert an episode, by way of a preface to the English translation, that brings my *Prophecies* back to me, after a long voyage at sea: from the other side of the Atlantic, whence everything departed, from Melville's country.

———

I WOULD HAVE WANTED—this was a dream—to write by way of a preface a kind of short treatise on all the warnings and prefaces addressed to the reader that mark the history of literature as well as the history of philosophy. From the "idle reader" of *Don Quixote*'s Prologue all the way to Borges's "preface of prefaces" (in his *Prólogos con un prólogo de prólogos*), through the famous apostrophe by Baudelaire, at the beginning of *Flowers of Evil* ("Hypocrite reader,— fellowman,—my twin") or the preface to the *Phenomenology of Spirit* by Hegel, which Derrida commented upon in his "Hors livre" for *Dissemination*, another preface on prefaces . . .

More modestly, and before letting the *Prophecies* speak of and for themselves (yes: *of and for themselves*), I will be content to try to read one of those innumerable addresses to the reader that open the books we read. Only one preface, then—of which I will attempt a gloss that should serve as a preface. It is the Preface to a singular treatise John Donne composed in 1608. Here is its complete title: "*Biathanatos. A Declaration of that Paradox or Thesis, that Self-Homicide is not so naturally Sin that it may never be otherwise; wherein the Nature and the Extent of all those Laws which seem to be violated by this Act are diligently surveyed.*[2] Why call upon this work here? Perhaps in order to speak again, if otherwise, that of which the *Prophecies* do not cease speaking: *reading is death*. Reading is, in effect, the moment when the end of the text is announced. It is the prophecy of its end, which seals and beheads it at the same time: the text capitalizes itself in reading while losing its heading or its head. *Reading is death—of the text*: such could have been the title of *Prophecies*. Announcing nothing but the survival, which is to say, the promise of that which remains to come, of the text. It is because it dies and does not cease dying—committing suicide even—in reading that the text signals toward its future to come, not, however, toward an eternal or immortal survival, but rather *toward its very finitude*.

But let us turn toward this *Biathanatos* by John Donne, toward this apology for suicide that Borges contributed to saving from oblivion by dedicating a short essay to it in his 1952 *Other Inquisitions*. As well, in homage to Jacques Derrida and to his thought, which has accompanied me throughout the pages that follow, I would like to be able to translate Donne's title as "life-death [*la vie–la mort*]."

HERE IS A FIRST PASSAGE from the Preface that, preceding the reading of *Biathanatos* it nonetheless engages already, speaks at least as much *of* the reader as *to* the reader.

> If, therefore, of readers, which Gorionides observes to be of four sorts—sponges, which attract all without distinguishing; hourglasses, which receive and pour out as fast; bags, which retain only the dregs of the spices and let the wine escape; and sieves, which retain the best only—I find some of the last sort, I doubt not but they may be hereby enlightened. (*The Preface declaring the reasons, the purpose, the way, and the end of the Author*, 43)

The good reader would thus be a sifter, a sieve to filter the text and ensure that only bits of it—and the best among them—survive. Yet reading might be a quasi-transcendental for the text: it is reading that enables it to exist. Reading is at bottom the condition of possibility of the text, but a condition inscribed within it. Henceforth, to say that it is the text itself and before all that at its core disposes and configures the place of reading is to locate the reading outside of it within it, in it but out of it: a kind of crypt (a double enclosure, as I call it in *Prophecies*) in which the text, each time, *reads itself*. Which is to say that it filters itself or absorbs itself, fills itself or empties itself of itself. In short, in these *leaks* that traverse it (as if the text were saying of itself, much like Captain Ahab in the Leviathan-text of *Moby-Dick*: "I am all aleak myself"), the text loses itself in order to guard itself; it dies in order to live; it lives from its death, *within itself*.

On the title page of *Biathanatos*, there appears a citation, or rather, a free adaptation extracted from the prologue to John of Salisbury's *Policraticus* (ca. 1115–80): "Non omnia vera esse profiteor. / Sed Legentium usibus inservire [whether it is true or false, it will serve the reader as useful]."[3] Donne's own work thus introduces itself under the sign of fiction (even of the *fiction of fiction*, to the extent that this epigraph, borrowed from another, commits *neither* to falsity *nor* to veracity with regard to what follows), but a *useful* fiction, which is to say, one that will have *effects*. An effective fiction, as it were, or better yet: *effictive*.[4] This effictivity, this performativity of fiction in effects, does not concern the reader alone, upon whom it is supposed to act so that he reconsider the value of suicide. It concerns first of all the text itself. Better yet: it concerns the text insofar as *its* life and *its* death are at stake in the fact that it *reads itself*. This is what Donne enunciates very clearly in the first dedicatory epistle, which follows the title page.

Before we come to that, though, let me briefly point out that, in the modern edition of *Biathanatos*, there are between the title page and the Preface not one but three dedications. The first two were written in the author's hand, at a time when the book existed only in manuscript form. The third (a letter by Donne's son "To the Right Honorable, the Lord Philip Herbert") recalls that *Biathanatos* was not published during Donne's lifetime. It was published only in 1647, that is, sixteen years after his death and against his wishes, by his son.

Let us read the first epistle then, in which the author and father of this still-unpublished text addresses himself to "the noblest knight, Sir Edward Herbert." There he declares: "Sir, I make account that this book hath enough performed that which it undertook, both by argument and example. It shall, therefore, the less need to be itself another example of the doctrine. It shall not, therefore, kill itself, that is, not bury itself; for if it should do so, those reasons by which that act should be defended or excused were also lost with it." A cursory reading will see here an elegant or affected manner of saying that the author of the manuscript wishes for it to survive, even if he does not wish for its publication. But upon re-reading, these abyssal sentences articulate a double, undecidable injunction: that the text serve as example; that it not serve as example.

An example of what?

An example of doctrine, of course, regarding this apology for suicide that the text illustrates, defends, and enunciates. But also, indissociably (since one example comes to contaminate the other), an example of itself or in itself; an example of its own mortality or textual finitude.

It is this same fold [*pli ou repli*] of the question of the suicide of the text itself that one can see at work in the third dedicatory epistle, in which John Donne, Jr., reminds the reader that the treatise is not the work of his own hand but must be attributed to his father. This third allographic dedication thus calls upon a double authority—that of the father and that of the lord to whom the work is dedicated. Or rather, and more precisely, it calls upon the sovereign authority of the latter in order to protect the writing in the place of the former, who is dead. It does so even to justify that the writing live again in printed form against the will of his dead father; in order to make it survive *beyond the death* of its author, therefore, and in order to take care for this survival.

Yet the life and death of the text, which are thereby announced, seem reciprocally to contaminate one another at the very moment of dispatch—they haunt each other under the quill of the son.

My Lord, although I have not exactly obeyed your commands, yet I hope I have exceeded them, by presenting to your Honor this treatise which is so much the better by being not mine own, and may therefore, peradventure, deserve to live for facilitating the issues of death. It was written long since by my father, and by him forbid both the press and the fire; neither had I subjected it now to the public view, but that I could find no certain way to defend it from the one but by committing it to the other. For . . . two dangers appeared more eminently to hover over this, being then a manuscript: a danger of being utterly lost, and a danger of being utterly found and fathered by some of those wild atheists who, as if they came into the world by conquest, . . . are resolved to be learned. . . . Your Lordship's protection will defend this innocent from these two monsters, men that cannot write and men that cannot read; and, I am very confident, all those that can will think it may deserve this favour from your Lordship. For although this book appears under the notion of a paradox, yet I desire your Lordship to look upon this doctrine as a firm and established truth: *Da vida osar morir.* Your Lordship's most humble servant, John Donne.

*Daring to die gives life*: this phrase—this already abyssal sentence, in which life and death are not opposed but appear to nourish each other infinitely—this maxim will certainly be pertinent to readers, beginning with the addressee of the dedication, who will be able to, or have to, apply it to the conduct of their existence after reading the short, fictitious, or fictively fictitious treatise that follows. However, according to a complication that comes to reproduce the reciprocal implication of life and death, this enunciation seems to have to be applied first of all to the text itself, which it thus announces and introduces. This treatise, which is not his own, says John Donne, Jr., in effect, "may therefore, peradventure, deserve to live" *for* (because, to the extent that) "facilitating the issues of death."

Once again, and as in the first autograph dedication, it is not only in its content, subject, or theme that the writing co-implicates in this manner, by complicating them abyssally, life and death. It is as text, by being born as text, that it is already itself implicated in this complication. Let us reread, in fact, Donne, Jr.

The treatise, he says, which his father forbade "both the press and the fire," is now subjected to "the public view" by the filial signatory of the dedication to the lord. It is published, therefore, beginning to live, but thereby risking death *for this very reason*: Donne, Jr., claims to have found "no certain way to defend it from the one," that is, from fire and destruction, "but by committing to the other," which is to say, to this *other death* that publication is, public appearance, becoming-text before the law of publicity. Irremediably, the manuscript, just about to appear [*de paraître ou de comparaître*] as text in the public space, oscillates between two threats: "a danger of being utterly lost, and a danger of being utterly found."

In short, the text gives itself to be read by daring death in order to live. Or: it escapes death by fire or by oblivion only by dying otherwise. In order to live.

———

BEFORE *BIATHANATOS*, Donne, Sr., had entitled one of his *Paradoxes and Problems* "That All Things Kill Themselves." There he asserted that "to affect, yea to effect their owne *death*, all living things are importun'd." With *Biathanatos*, the self-crucifixion of Christ (an idea owed apparently to John of Apamea in the fifth century) is transformed into an affirmation that *suicide* is the founding concept of Christianity.[5] But as we have seen, while reading the dedication to Lord Herbert, it is also the text that, for Donne, Jr., presents itself as an *autobiothanatography*, which is to say, as a writing that lives from its own death.

Mutatis mutandis, if Leviathan is the text, as I try to repeat over and over with Melville in *Prophecies*, one must remember that this allegory or this symbol borrowed from Hobbes is first of all a "mortal god," as Carl Schmitt enjoyed recalling. This paradoxical expression cannot be heard otherwise than as having Christological antecedents: the son (the text) sacrifices itself so that the father (the text) lives.

And the reader in all of this?

The reader would be a site of sorts for this life of the text as a survival that is haunted by its own death, a site where the text can live and die, abyssally, a site that is therefore the condition of possibility of its *finite survival*. But a site that, following a topography that defies all simple logic, also inhabits the text from within, marks and remarks itself there.

Is this to say that reading would be the transubstantiation, by ingestion, *of* the text? Perhaps, but on condition that one hears well the dual meaning of this genitive: *of* the text, yes, on the one hand, in the sense that the text is this object that readers ingest while reading it; and *of* the text, on the other hand, in the sense that the text is the subject of its own autothanatographical digestion, with all the meteoric phenomena that can thereby ensue (as I try to show in *Prophecies*).[6] Be that as it may, the figure of reading as *digestion*, with its Christological echoes, is invoked many times by Donne:[7] for example, in his Preface, when just after he borrowed from Gorionides his quadruple typology of readers (sponges, broken glasses, bags, or sieves), he continues: "And as the eyes of Eve were opened by the taste of the apple, though it be said, before that she saw the beauty of the tree, so the digesting of this may, though not present fair objects, yet bring them to see the nakedness and deformity of their own reasons, founded upon a rigorous suspicion." Reading, in sum, will open the eyes. It will allow seeing, revealing truth to readers who make the text live by letting it die: by ingesting it and digesting it, by carrying it within themselves, transubstantiated.

More than ever, with Donne's *Biathanatos* the premises of a deconstruction of Christianity (as understood by Jean-Luc Nancy) seem closely woven with those of a general deconstruction, as broached in its founding enunciation, of which *Prophecies* is perhaps no more than a long commentary: *il n'y a pas de hors-texte*.

Another way of saying that the text begins by devouring itself (committing suicide). In itself.

———————— • ————————

BUT (THEN), there is a remainder.

Something indigestible.

And that is why one must *reread*.

In fact, Donne, Sr., before the Pre(post)face of the son, was already making use of the metaphor (if it is simply one) of digestion. This is so in "Distinction I," which opens the first part ("Of Law and Nature"). There, naming for the first time the object of his treatise, namely, "self-homicide," Donne writes: "which to be sin everybody hath so sucked, and digested, and incorporated into the body of his faith and religion, . . . so that none brings the metal now to the test, nor touch . . . yet . . . we must . . . preposterously examine: first, why this fact should be so resolutely condemned, and why there should be this precipitation in our judgement to pronounce this, above all other sins, irremissible" (45)."

One will have to read, therefore, to make read and reread—*Biathanatos* will apply itself to it—scriptures, their commentators, the Fathers of the Church, the moralists, the philosophers; to read and reread in order to demonstrate that to give death, to *take one's life* [*se donner la mort*], is an act that "may be free, not only from enormous degrees of sin, but of all" (46). In the end, it is the *autothanatographical* dimension of the text that will end up buttressed or legally founded: if the text, like so many willful martyrs, takes its own life *in and by itself* (for such is its suicide), it is in order to remain still and always to come, in order to survive like a living dead. A phantom or an undigestible specter, to whom one cannot grant, finally and whatever Donne may say, absolution or eternity, for it is condemned to wander and to return without cease, without peace or reconciliation.

Dedicated, in sum, to *remain—ended*.

Paris, June 2007–July 2008

# LIMINARY NOTE

IN A FIRST VERSION, *the pages that follow were intended to serve as the material (the "libretto") for a musical spectacle by Georges Aperghis:* Storm Warning [Avis de tempête] *(created November 17, 2004, at the Opera of Lille, France).*

*I would not know how to express my gratitude for his having taken me on this adventure, one to which he himself has given the form of a stunning score of "musical theater" (a genre of which he has the secret), whereas I have given it the form of the essay that follows. He has been its first reader, and its instigator.*

*P. S.*

# Prophecies of Leviathan

READING PAST MELVILLE

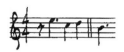

# The Double Enclosure

WHAT DAY IS IT TODAY?

Today, the day of today.

And how will I manage to hold you back? How will I become this Scheherazade, who, close to you, will postpone the next day of every day that comes?

I could trust in fortune, in the casting of lots.

Here is a tale. Listen.

I begin *here*. I begin, that is, where, today, the book will have opened, as if by chance, at this page.

The narrator, who took it into his head "to go on a whaling voyage," imagines his project as "part of a grand programme of Providence that was drawn up a long time ago" (1:7). He dreams that his design, were it to be realized, will be like a performance in the greatest circus in the world, "a sort of brief interlude and solo" between "more extensive" events. He sees himself already, in advance, on the posters, his own little story announced between the lines of the greater story or history.[1]

"I take it," he says, "that this part of the bill must have run something like this," look:

> "*Grand Contested Election for the Presidency of the United States.*
> "WHALING VOYAGE BY ONE ISHMAEL.
> "BLOODY BATTLE IN AFFGHANISTAN."

The tale I am reading to you is dated 1851. *Moby-Dick* is more than 150 years old.[2] And yet it seems to me that here, under our eyes, Ishmael the narrator would have inscribed in advance on the great poster of the world a chain of events destined to be repeated, as if stuttering, very close to us, in a yesterday so proximate that its consequences still resonate everywhere, to this very day:

> *"Grand Contested Election for the Presidency of the United States.*
>
> "BLOODY BATTLE IN AFFGHANISTAN."

Such would have been the program.

And then what? What tomorrow and the next day? Will I be able to read it in this tale, as if in a book of oracles, to read what awaits us? Or, failing that, will I at least be able to read in it the assurance of a future awaiting, indeed, of a promise of what I hardly and reluctantly dare call *us*, you and me?

Surely, no.

But there will have been, *today*, the possibility of a reading that one should not be afraid of calling *prophetic*, in spite of everything.

It is about this that I want to speak with you. And with it that I entertain the hope of keeping you, of holding you back again and again, in and through reading as prophecy, as promise of a future to come.

This minute and barely graspable chance, which I hang onto as one holds onto a buoy in the ocean, would itself depend on something like a double enclosure.

1. One finds in *Moby-Dick* that poster you just saw, which seems to announce the program of a tragic event to come, and for us already occurred. Thus, our recent history would have been contained, enclosed in advance in the ancient history of this fiction that is Melville's novel.

2. But on this same poster, the tale of *Moby-Dick* (to wit, this "whaling voyage by one Ishmael") is itself presented as enclosed, that is to say, included and framed *between* the two

events posted, which we have just lived through: a contested American election and the war in Afghanistan. The tale of *Moby-Dick* would be in turn as if enclosed between two milestones of our recent history.

I do not tire of looking at this poster—

> *"Grand Contested Election for the Presidency of the United States.*
> "WHALING VOYAGE BY ONE ISHMAEL.
> "BLOODY BATTLE IN AFFGHANISTAN."

It inscribes history in the text and the text in history, the text in the story. And this structure, in the shape of a double enclosure, fascinates me—Is it what calls upon the fiction of a prophetic reading, through this incredible temporal knot, according to which *Moby-Dick* would contain and enclose the program of the world to come, which would itself contain and enclose the program of *Moby-Dick*?

You already understand that it is not, for me, a matter of demonstrating to you that there is here an accomplished prophecy as such. (Melville has not predicted anything in this sense, neither the election *in extremis* of George Bush, Jr., nor Afghanistan and the Taliban, nor all the tragedies that are unfolding under our eyes at this very moment.) It is, rather, a matter of thinking a kind of *propheticity*, which, in reading, remains to come like an open possibility, perhaps like the future itself. Like a promise, or better: a *prophecy of prophecy.* Postponed.

## "I"

I will begin reading again, to begin with. I will then begin again, again and again, every evening to come, in order to hold you back.

But wherefrom will I begin? I could entertain you with Melville's more overt political tales, with *White-Jacket*, for example, which, while describing the power relations on a war vessel, seems to announce the American Civil War; or else with "Billy Budd, Sailor," this "internal narrative," whose hero sails first on a ship named *The Rights of Man*, before he too is called to serve on a war vessel . . .

But no, I would rather first let myself be guided by a kind of outline where the scene is radically reduced to a face-off between two characters: one close to the hearth, braving bad weather; the other arriving without warning, like an untimely storm.

To begin with, then, here is this fascinating short story by Melville entitled "The Lightning-Rod Man." I am going to read it to you unhurriedly, untying it line by line, paragraph by paragraph. And, as with the other tales I will divert for you later on, I shall not refrain from slowing down, from deferring, my own reading—as much as my strength, and yours, will permit—doing so by way of infinite parentheses, innumerable commentaries and glosses, all of which will perhaps engulf it, or drown it under a flood.

Listen, it is the beginning, the *incipit*:
"What grand irregular thunder, I thought, standing on my hearthstone . . ." (LRM, 118).

Observe the scene.

Slowly, something is going to happen to "I," to he who says "I," standing. And I would like, at the risk of still deferring its arrival, to show you how what happens to him occurs, how it arrives. Under what conditions comes that which is coming, while remaining to come; remaining to be read and read again

"I," then, stands stock-still and vertically, like the letter *I*, which, in English, names him or it: I. And this I thinks.

He thinks standing, watchful. He thinks standing, steady upon soil or sturdy stone, on the base of the hearthstone. Nor could he vacillate. His balance, his stance seems stable.

Straight as an I, I maintains itself vis-à-vis the storm that comes. Thus erected in his stand, I watches and thinks the storm from the hearth, from the focal point of the fireplace in which he seems to find his bearing.

Now, imagine that this I who is, in the text, watching and thinking the event of the storm that comes, imagine that this I is a letter of the text itself: *I*. Imagine that it is a *character*, after the fashion of those whom Melville, speaking of a copy of Shakespeare's *The Plays*, which he had acquired in February 1849, described in the following terms: "It is an edition in glorious great type, every letter whereof is a soldier, & the top of every 't' like a musket barrel."[3]

*I*—this would thus be a posture or an instance that, from within the text, looks and watches over what arrives in and by way of the text. *I* would be an eye, the large or small eye of a Cyclops blinking along the lines, in the midst of other letters that form, for themselves, words, sentences, and enunciations. *I*—a letter among others, yet observing and reading the others; a kind of sentry letter, looking out for the advent of the storm-text to come.

There is another short story by Melville of which *I* is the very first letter and the very first word. Detached, ahead of the text, which it precedes and watches over from the vantage point of its title: "I and My Chimney."

Here too, I is attached to the chimney hearth by a kind of fastening line (the conjunction *and*), which seems to extend long enough to tie them into a "we," into the first person and the semblance of a plural: "I and my chimney, two grey-headed old smokers, reside in the country. We are, I may say, old settlers here; particularly my old chimney, which settles more and more every day."[4]

But this "we," it is obvious, is not an I and a Thou; it is rather a doubling of an I in its place, and *as* its very place. The verticality of the chimney is simply an echo of the I, which seems to insure or sustain, in the manner of a stake or a prop, its erection and its settlement within its sovereign identity to itself.[5]

What will happen to this "I"? What could happen to it, in and through the event of a text of which it is, *to the letter*, already a part?

In "The Lightning-Rod Man," everything is as if I had already begun, inside the text, reading this very text, one which brings to the I the threatening event of a thunderstorm. Everything, then, is as if I were the eye, deciphering the hurricane that approaches. For I is evidently the narrator unrolling the text of the storm that comes, of which he is also the first reader. He is also the spectator who, in the text, watches the storm come from the tranquil assurance of his hearth.

"I" is therefore both the hearth and the focus [*foyer*] *of the text* and the hearth and focus *in the text*. In other words, I is the focal point of the narration from which the text invents itself and delivers itself over to reading. Yet it is also, at the same time, an anchor point that the text represents as stable ("standing on my hearthstone"), facing the storm that comes for it and by it.

How, henceforth, could this I be exposed to the arrival of a storm worthy of that name? How could it be exposed, that is, to the coming of an event that he would not expect, that would befall him from outside? What could ever occur, unprecedented, in what he himself is producing and reading?

In fact, although the storm has already broken out, it remains (it will remain still) to come in order truly to arrive, in order to touch this I, to affect this I steadily poised upon, moored or fastened to his hearthstone. In order to *sweep him away*, the storm will have to repeat itself, in the reverberation of its own provenance: it will have to be *re-sounding* in order, finally, to break down the focal anchoring of an eye that has already begun reading it, awaiting it therefore, expecting it.

In short, the real storm will play itself out in the reading that is already at play in the text. Which is why it will not only be a matter of my reading to you a tale about a storm, as the object or theme of a narration. Rather, reading itself will have to become stormy and tempestuous—so that there might be some unpredictability, some *unprereadability.*

Expect, therefore, a *reading storm*. Can you feel its downpour, its surge?

# The Event, or Reading Without Heading

FROM THE BEGINNING OF "The Lightning-Rod Man," the elements are raging. "The scattered bolts boomed overhead and crashed down among the valleys, every bolt followed by zig-zag irradiations, and swift slants of sharp rain, which audibly rang, like a charge of spear-points, on my low shingled roof" (LRM, 118).

And, in the turmoil of this storm that sounds and resounds, there are drawn tracks, arrows, lines. One, the vertical of the lightning, is the axis upon which appear together, that is to say, *co-appear [comparaissent]*, in their face to face, both I and the storm. The horizontal of the roof of the house doubles that of the ground, that of the base of the hearthstone. And the oblique, the diagonal streaks of the rain, the angles of the lightning bolts, all come to unhinge with their hatchings, as it were, the abscissa and ordinates thus defined.

What is brewing here could therefore resemble a scene of reading. In it, the erect and sovereign eye of the narrator reading (I, eye) is like a beacon sustained by the horizontal lines upon which it comes to rest in order to find a foothold. It is confronted with zigzags, with the angular motions that confuse markers and expectations at the horizon. It would be, in short, a reading in the form of angled lines, a reading whose linearity would break down, zigzagging among lightning bolts and resounding thunderclaps.

I can see coming from afar, very far, the unhinged axes of a prophetic reading that would proceed by way of spectacular bursts [*par coups d'éclat*].

It is on the complex articulation of these very lines—vertical, horizontal and diagonal—that a certain Father Mapple insists most particularly, in the sermon he delivers on the book of the prophet Jonah (in chapter 9 of *Moby-Dick*). Listen to him as he speaks from the pulpit; hear his reading the Bible out loud, in which he seeks to captivate the faithful.

What does the visionary Jonah see, asks Father Mapple, what does he see as he lays upon his berth, on board the docking ship that will carry him off to Tarshish?

> Screwed at its axis against the side, a swinging lamp slightly oscillates . . . the lamp, flame and all, though in slight motion, still maintains a permanent obliquity with reference to the room; though, in truth, infallibly straight itself, it but made obvious the false, lying levels among which it hung. The lamp alarms and frightens Jonah; as lying in his berth his tormented eyes roll round the place, and this thus far successful fugitive finds no refuge for his restless glance. . . . The floor, the ceiling, and the side, all are awry. "Oh! So my conscience hangs in me!" he groans, "straight upward, so it burns; but the chambers of my soul are all in crookedness!" (9:44–45)

Jonah the prophet looks around. Or perhaps he too is tempted to read and decipher that which comes (it will, by the way, later turn out to be a storm). But the coordinates of his reading are blurred. In the turmoil of his soul, something threatens verticality, the erection of his conscience. The source of his light is not straight; the eye of his spirit vacillates and renders the lines of the horizon uncertain, untrustworthy.

Moreover, unlike the erected I of "The Lightning-Rod Man," Jonah finds himself in a horizontal position: lying in his bed. Jonah might as well be sleeping or dreaming, even dreaming awake; he is, at any rate, not standing upright as he faces an event that comes, which he would be sovereignly observing.

In fact, Jonah is, rather, in the process of avoiding what has already reached him, namely, God's command, saying to him: "Get up, go to Nineveh, that great city" (Jon. 3:2). Jonah was afraid of it, and he ran away. He is thus himself as if suspended between "the word of the Lord," from which he flees, and its repetition to come in the storm that will punish his flight once he will have taken to the sea. Jonah runs ahead of an event—or a call—that has already befallen him, that follows him and will end up catching up with him in order to reach him anew, in the form of a thunderstorm, during the crossing for which he boarded ship. He runs, at top speed, in order to escape the verticality of "the word of the Lord," which struck down on him like lightning. He shirks from this "Get up" enjoining him to stand up and rise, to respond in the affirmative by saying "I." The obliqueness of the lie—for Jonah is lying—in which the space surrounding him is henceforth revealed to him (he who is lying), this obliqueness is nothing else, perhaps, than the reflection of his flight in front of the uprightness required of him. Between the punctual instant of God's command, which occurs at just the right time, and its repetition in the storm that awaits the prophet lying in the bed of his dreams and nightmares there is a diagonal axis, a line of flight where nothing is certain, where a long wait looms with no guarantee of a horizontal or of a horizon.

Now, I would like to head out with you toward writing and reading as these narratives represent them, about which I will speak to you in order to hold you back. Heading, then, for a sailing without heading, lost at sea without compass, and yet still magnetized.

What I can already predict to you is that the appearance of Father Mapple reading and interpreting the story of Jonah will be mistreated. It will no longer be possible *to anchor* reading and to safely reach one's destination, as the minister tells his own flock: "Beloved shipmates, clinch the last verse of the first chapter of Jonah" (9:42). There will not even be bodyguards, perhaps, no more railings, nor any of these connecting strands to which Father Mapple can entrust his journey across a text. "Shipmates," he says as well, the book of Jonah "is one of the smallest strands in the mighty cable of the Scriptures. Yet what depths of the soul does Jonah's deep sea-line sound!" (ibid.).

As soon as the anchors could drift off and the cables break, the distinction will no longer be assured, in reading, between surface and depth, between illusion—or deceit—and truth. But here, perhaps, opens a space which is not that of verifiable prophecy, which is rather that of the infinite promise, extending beyond the horizon. This is, perhaps, where what awaits us is neither confirmed prophecies nor those awaiting confirmation, but rather prophecies of prophecies, in which waiting itself is making us wait.

But quiet!—someone, some I, close to the hearth, enjoins us to listen. For he too stretches his ear.

# The Aura of the Weather

HERE IS IN FACT someone arriving, someone unknown, who seems carried off or brought on by the storm: "Hark!—someone at the door. Who is this that chooses a time of thunder for making calls?" (LRM, 118).

Faced with this untimely and tempestuous arrival, the question asked by the narrator close to the hearth strangely resembles this other one: "[Kent]—Who's there, besides foul weather?"[6]

As if, in the middle of a thunderstorm, the arriving one was hardly separable from the weather he "chooses," from the weather itself.

The weather he chooses?

In fact, the narrator's question ("Who is this that *chooses* a time of thunder?") is already a curious one. Why assume that the one arriving has *chosen* his time or his weather [*son temps*]? And why also suppose that he is *making* calls? Would it not have been more plausible to conjecture that the unknown one who comes is lost in the storm, that he is forced to look for a refuge, surprised by the rain?

In its formulation, the question thus introduces, if in a roundabout way, the foreboding feeling that what is pushing or driving the visitor are not the raging elements and that he is instead the agent and *maker*, that it is he who has, as it were, sent them as scouts. The lightning and thunderbolts would be a kind of *avant-garde* of his arrival. They will have announced him like portent signs. In a sort of future anterior, they will have constituted his *aura*.[7]

# Before Sight, the Voice

THE ONE ARRIVING is behind the door. He knocks:

"And why don't he, man-fashion, use the knocker, instead of making that doleful undertaker's clatter with his fist against the hollow panel?" (LRM, 118).

Prior to being seen—already announced by the turmoil that will have preceded him, but without being, for all that, expected—the visitor is heard.

This advance of the ear ("organ of fear," of "night" or of "twilight," according to Nietzsche), this antecedence of hearing in relation to sight (the narrator first hears a "clatter," a series of noises bristling with alliterations in the key of *k*) could announce the nonhuman: ahuman or inhuman or, yet, superhuman. It could be the signal of an approach by a being not made after the fashion of man, "man-fashion."

It is this advance that, in *Moby-Dick*, announces to Ishmael and to Queequeg (his "savage" companion) the ghostly return of a certain Elijah—a figure of prophecy, if there ever was one—whom we will meet more than once: "'Avast!' cried a voice, whose owner at the same time coming close behind us, laid a hand upon both our shoulders. . . . It was Elijah" (21:98).

Before he is a face or even a name, Elijah the prophet is first of all a voice here, a call. As for what or who, in the middle of the storm, comes knocking at the door in "The Lightning-Rod Man"—it is also only noise or "clatter." Must one open? Must one welcome the rumor of ill omen? Or rather: What will happen if I, if the eye of the text, opens (and opens itself) to what or who comes to inscribe and carve in his hearth and home a *center of intrusion* (as one speaks of a "center of infection")?

# Outside—Inside

SINCE THE HOST opened the door to him, the stranger arriving is now "planted," standing stock-still in the middle of the room. He is erect, firm and immobile, right at the center, as if near a second hearth or counter-hearth: "His sunken pitfalls of eyes were ringed by indigo halos, and played with an innocuous sort of lightning: the gleam without the bolt. The whole man was dripping. He stood in a puddle on the bare oak floor; his strange walking-stick vertically resting at his side" (LRM, 118–19).

The stranger relays, he repeats, the thunderstorm; he reflects it or doubles it. The storm thus continues outside and inside, in the eyes of the visitor. He is arriving, dripping like a miniature flood, spreading in the very home, at the hearth, the aqueous meteors he has imported from without.[8] He unleashes within what arrives—what has already arrived—without.

Like that stranger, Father Mapple also incarnates, over the course of his sermon on Jonah, the resounding doubling of the outside within.

His preaching takes place, in fact, during a storm. "I fought my way against the stubborn storm," says Ishmael the narrator just before entering the chapel where he has come to listen to the sermon (7:34). When Father Mapple finally enters in his turn, putting an end to the wait of the faithful, he also brings with him a flood: "his tarpaulin hat ran down with melting sleet, and his great pilot cloth jacket seemed almost to drag him to the floor with the weight of the water it had absorbed" (8:38). Thus carrying the outside within, much as he carries faith into the heart of the faithful, the Father himself becomes, during his sermon, a kind of internal storm, an enclosure of the thunderstorm raging outside.

> While he was speaking these words, the howling of the shrieking, slanting storm without seemed to add new power to the preacher, who, when describing Jonah's sea-storm, seemed tossed by a storm himself. His deep chest heaved as with a ground-swell; his tossed arms seemed the warring elements at work; and the thunders that rolled away from his swarthy brow, and the light leaping from his eye, made all his simple hearers look on him with a quick fear that was strange to them. (9:47)

In relation to the stranger of "The Lightning-Rod Man," how-ever, Father Mapple cuts a much more abyssal figure of the enclo-sure. Not only does he repeat in his own body the storm raging outside the chapel; not only does he make it resonate within the chapel's walls. He also doubles this very repetition when he narrates, in order to carve it on the heart of his audience, the storm sent upon Jonah by God.

(I will speak to you again of Jonah, as himself a figure of the enclosure. For one meets Jonah often enough in Melville. Not only in *Moby-Dick* but also in the adventures of *Israel Potter*, for example: "And here in the black bowels of the ship, sunk low in the sunless sea, our poor Israel lay for a month, like Jonah in the belly of the whale"; *IP*, 3:15)

# Naming and Meteoromancy

THE STRANGER, of whom we will later learn that he is a traveling salesman selling lightning rods, has no name. Besides, at no point will the host himself seek to know the *proper* name of his visitor. He does not ask him to identify himself. It is rather he, the host, who names or *nicknames* [surnomme] him.

> "Sir," said I, bowing politely, "have I the honor of a visit from that illustrious god, Jupiter Tonans? So stood he in the Greek statue of old, grasping the lightning-bolt. If you be he, or his viceroy, I have to thank you for this noble storm you have brewed among your mountains. Listen: That was a glorious peal. Ah, to a lover of the majestic, it is a good thing to have the Thunderer himself in one's cottage. The thunder grows finer for that." (LRM, 119)

The stranger is thus given a surname or nickname, *Jupiter Tonans*, which likens him to the meteoric figure par excellence, namely, Captain Ahab, who, in *Moby-Dick*, is himself nicknamed "Old Thunder" by the "old sailor chaps." This Ishmael learns from the strange and troubling character named Elijah (19:92).

Besides, Ahab, the very name Ahab, is also presented as a kind of nickname when it becomes the object of an explicit gloss by Captain Peleg, owner of the whaling ship. Ahab is, of course, a biblical name.[9] "Ahab of old, thou knowest, was a crowned king!" explains Peleg to Ishmael, before offering a strange detail: "Captain Ahab did not name himself. 'Twas a foolish, ignorant whim of his crazy, widowed mother, who died when he was only a twelvemonth old. And yet . . . the name would somehow prove prophetic" (16:79).

This is indeed a strange thing, for who, after all, what child of man, has ever named himself? In this sense, every name is an improper name. It is always in advance a surname or nickname. Would there be in this onomastic prosthesis of the origin, which constitutes every nomination, would there be found in this substitutive, initial *surnomination*, the source of the propheticity of names?

This is what seems to be indicated by the ancient practice of "meteoromancy," to which the *Encyclopédie* of Diderot and d'Alembert dedicates an article, where one can read the following:

> Divination by way of meteors; and since igneous meteors are those which incite the most fear among men, *meteoromancy* most properly designates divination by way of thunder and lightning. . . . Seneca teaches us that two serious authors, who had served as magistrates, had written on this matter. It even seems that one of them exhausted the matter thoroughly, since he gave a precise list of the different kinds of thunder. *He classified both their names and the prognostics that could be deduced from them*, doing so with an air of confidence even more striking than the things he was reporting. (emphasis added)[10]

Naming, nicknaming, storms and "old thunders": this ancient tradition seems to have been passed on from meteoromancy to the modern meteorology with which we are familiar.

Thus, in the eighteenth century, hurricanes bore the name of the patron saint of the day on which they occurred. In Puerto Rico, for example, on July 26, 1825, there was Santa Ana. Then, on September 13, 1876, San Felipe, which returned in 1928 on the same day of the same month: the same but another, doubling the first of which he bore the name. San Felipe anew, San Felipe the second, the *revenant*, which made thousands of victims.

Later, hurricanes came to carry the names of women, short names, these, and easy to remember. So Alice, on May 25, 1953. And the same year: Barbara, Carol, Dolly, Edna. Then, some alternation was introduced with masculine first names. On even years, men would start: Allen, Alberto, Arthur . . . On uneven years, women: Ana, Arlene, Alicia . . . In alphabetical order.[11]

Meteorologists, who predict every day the weather or the catastrophes to come, now have at their disposal six lists that, every six years, rotate. The year 2000 will therefore see some of the specters of 1994 return; 2001 those of 1989 and 1995. And all of these will return again in 2007. It is written and inscribed; it is prescribed, in this *meteoronomastics*, which programs their ghostly returns [*revenance*].[12]

By its baptismal act, by the force of its nomination and the attribution of nicknames, a storm would be but an enclosure of time: an event already included and framed between its anticipation of itself and its consecutiveness upon itself.

In at least one of the great tractates that mark out the history of meteoromantic divination, in Cicero's *De Divinatione*, prophecy made from the weather is compared to navigation, on the one hand, and to exegetical reading, on the other.

The *De Divinatione* takes the form of a dialogue between Cicero (Marcus is his first name) and his elder brother, Quintus. Marcus reports at length the words of Quintus (these take up the entirety of book 1) as a defense and illustration of oracular practice. He then dedicates book 2 to his own response and point-by-point refutation.

It is in the voice of Quintus, therefore, that a first analogy is enunciated, between the failure of prophecy and shipwreck:

"But," it is objected, "sometimes predictions [*praedicta*] are made which do not occur [*eveniunt*]." . . . Surely the practice of medicine is an art, yet how many mistakes it makes! And what? Do navigators not also make mistakes? [*Quid? Gubernators none falluntur?*] . . . Did the fact that so many illustrious captains and kings suffered shipwreck [*naufragium*], deprive navigation of its right to be called an art [*artem gubernandi*]?[13]

One would think that Quintus is speaking of Ahab, of this mad navigator who bears the name of a king and exercises his art by governing the helm and leading his crew toward a mortal end. Yet further on Quintus also says that the "interpreters [*interpretes*]" of all

oracular signs—among which thunder and lightning are promi-
nent—are like "grammarians" who interpret "the poets" [*ut gram-
matici poetarum*].[14]

Reading, according to Quintus, would mean prophesying while
constantly risking a shipwreck. Would it also be to lose oneself and
drown oneself in signs, at the risk of never rising again within the
stability of a known sense?

# Prosthesis and Prophecy

THERE IS, I have just discovered, a proximate, contiguous relation between "The Lightning-Rod Man" and *Israel Potter*. Melville published the latter in serial form, which is to say, in installments, in *The Putnam's Monthly*. The second installment, in which Melville introduced the character of Benjamin Franklin into the narrative, was published in the August 1854 issue, in the pages immediately following "The Lightning-Rod Man," also published there for the first time.[15] Melville appears to have used the same source for both works, namely, *Letters and Papers on Electricity*, by Benjamin Franklin.

But Franklin also makes a brief and singular appearance in *Moby-Dick*. While defending the reputation of the whale hunters, Ishmael the narrator notes that those coming from Nantucket—this small island from which he will leave to hunt the white whale on board the *Pequod*—"have something better than royal blood" running in their veins, since they are kin to the inventor of the lightning rod: "The grandmother of Benjamin Franklin was Mary Morell; afterwards, by marriage, Mary Folger, one of the old settlers of Nantucket, and the ancestress to a long line of Folgers and harpooners—all kith and kin to noble Benjamin—this day darting the barbed iron from one side of the world to the other" (24:111).

Much as lineage binds the harpooners of Nantucket to Benjamin Franklin, would there be a kind of kinship between the harpoon (which carries with it a fishing line destined to haul the whale to the ship) and the lightning rod (which carries the igneous meteors that fall from the sky to the earth)?

I am thinking of Quintus here and of his analogy between divination, navigation, and reading, and so I ask myself: Where am I leading us by reading these lines? What are we going to fish, and at the risk of what striking, indeed, thundering shipwreck? Have we—we readers who trust we are standing close to the helm as "I" stands by his hearthstone—have we boarded a vessel bound for a voyage as disastrous as Ahab's?

In *Israel Potter* (this novel that travels so close to the story of "the lightning-rod man"), the hero is "harassed day and night, hunted . . . driven from hole to hole like a fox in the woods" before he is advised "to apply . . . for a berth as a laborer in the King's gardens," at the service of George III of England (*IP*, 5:29).

Israel, however, is a fugitive in enemy country. During the War of Independence in the American colonies, in 1774, he enlists as a sailor on the vessel *Washington*. Captured and imprisoned, he is subsequently taken to England, where he manages to escape. This is why it seems to him quite "curious" that "the very den of the British lion, the private grounds of the British king" could serve as "his securest asylum." He nonetheless follows the advice given him "by one whose sincerity he could not doubt" (ibid.).

He is finally "installed" there as "keeper of certain less private plants and walks" of the king's garden. He often sees the king "through intervening foliage," taking "some private but parallel walk," and has to repress regicidal temptation more than once, until one day he finds himself face to face with the king. Whether gifted with some "swift insight," or "whether some of the rumors prevailing outside of the garden had come to his ear" (5:31), the king immediately identifies Israel as "a Yankee" and a "runaway prisoner-of-war." Speaking in a curious mix of divinatory assurance and stammering hesitation, the king says to Israel: "you have sought this place to be safe from pursuit, eh? eh? Is it not so?—eh? eh? eh?"

The monarch stammers. "Well, ye're an honest rebel—rebel, yes, rebel," and he adds, still addressing Israel, "Hark ye, hark. Say nothing of this talk to any one. And hark again. . . . I shall see that you are safe—safe" (ibid.).

What is this stammering—a figure of repetition so close to the echo—a mark of in the royal elocution? Two forms of stammering have been clinically identified. The first is said to be *tonic* (i.e., a blocking that hinders emission) and the second *clonic* (i.e., the repeated iteration of a syllable or word). The king suffers more from the second form. He suffers from an iterative compulsion. His ailment is such that he repeats words; he *clones* them as soon as he utters them, which he does with great pains. The consequence of this singular and idiomatic impediment, this royal *idiotism*, which affects the sovereign, is the *prosthetic* character of his speech. Indeed, linguists have called *prosthesis* the addition, without semantic modification, of a letter or a syllable in front of a word's first letter.[16] As I read, I imagine that when the king, "in his rapid and half-stammering way," says to Israel: "You aint an Englishman,—no Englishman—no no," he pronounces in fact "En-Engl-Englishman," producing by proliferation of prosthetic cloning a word projected *forward* (toward the initial letter).

Stammering is thus a kind of echo that, rather and earlier than repetition (yes, *earlier*), precedes, *anticipates* with some concern the enunciation of a word-thing. Stammering is early rather than late (or perhaps the early and the late are, in it, inextricably mixed).

Is it a coincidence, therefore, if in *Israel Potter* and in *Moby-Dick* the two figures of divination that George III and Elijah are appear as if marked by the sign of stammering and by anticipating repetition? if their hypotheses become fore-theses, or better yet, *pro-theses?*

Elijah's speech in *Moby-Dick* is also suffused with staccato iterations that precisely seal and sign his prophetic character: "well, well, what's signed, is signed; and what's to be, will be," says he to Ishmael and Queequeg, whom he greets repeatedly, as if uttering a refrain, "morning to ye, shipmates, morning!" (19:93, in which the greeting also sounds like an anticipated *mourning*).

Jean Giono's French translation (which I have followed only from afar) does not render all the syllabic clones of the original. It occults and polishes—thus poorly reading—the stammering of the prophet. It misses the repetition that occurs when Elijah asks the two whalemen, "Shipmates, have ye shipped in that ship?" (19:91). Similarly, one must lend one's ear to the agitation, to the *clonus*—which is to say, in medical terms, to the rhythmic contraction—of Elijah's enunciation, shaken by the syllable *ye* (a form of address that also resonates in the anticipating "yet"): "Ye said true—ye hav'n't seen Old Thunder yet, have ye?" (19:92).

The most gripping crossing, however, between prophecy, pro-thesis and prosthesis can be found in the same chapter during the following exchange between Elijah the stranger and Ishmael, the latter being forced to concede that he has not yet seen Ahab:

> "He's sick they say, but is getting better and will be *all right* again before long."
>
> "*All right* again before long!" Laughed the stranger, with a solemnly derisive sort of laugh. "Look ye; when captain Ahab is *all right*, then this left arm of mine will be *all right*; not before." (ibid.; emphases added)

Once again, it is the jerked rhythmic, the sonic cloning of the word *right* that carries everything. One must read these sentences, which turn around a predictive diagnostic, around a kind of medical prophecy concerned with the health to come of Ahab the one-legged. In them, the word *right* is, as it were, dislocated from its sense by clonic iteration. Eliding one sense after another, one sense rather than another, Elijah opens an abyss in the word. When Ahab is all *right*, then the prophet's *left* arm will be *right* as well, all *right*. And, having found his address again, he too will be made *right*.

The senses (left and right) are confused, and the sense of the prediction is suspended. At the end, however, when the prosthetic Ahab with his ivory leg, far from ever rising from his mutilation by the white whale, leads his shipmates to their death, then, retrospectively, the prophecy of Elijah the prophet will have been verified.

It is necessary to remember here that, when Elijah appears at the beginning of the chapter, it is at arm's length that he *extends his pointing finger* toward the *Pequod*, the whaling ship Ishmael and Queequeg are about to board. Elijah demonstratively shows the ship twice. First, he levels "his massive fore-finger at the vessel in question" (the word *forefinger* evoking the entire array of prophetic terms and their suffix *fore*, from *foreseeing* to *foretelling*, *foreshadowing*, and so forth). Then, a few lines down: "'Aye, the Pequod—that ship there,' he said, drawing back his whole arm, and then rapidly shoving it straight out from him, with the fixed bayonet of his pointed finger darted full at the object" (19:91).

In this jerked, repetitive, and demonstrative gesture, the arm of Elijah the prophet points to its object as if by a gestural stammer. He *aims by repetition*, as an automatic rifle would when directed at a target in battle, with his finger transformed into a bayonet. And when the accuracy of his aim is verified, not only the content of his prediction but also his prophetic powers will be confirmed—his powers, which is to say, his ability to designate or to *point his finger* toward that which is coming: his own capacity to indicate (or yet again, as linguists would put it, his *indexicality*). *In fine*, the index of his hand will have been the darted arrow released at arm's length, *right* at the target.

I still have to mention to you an echoing repetition that, prior to the prophecy of the catastrophe announced by Elijah and its realization, reiterates in a properly monstrous fashion the scene of prosthetic and prophetic ostentation I have just read to you. This is chapter 100, entitled "Leg and Arm," in which the one-legged captain of the *Pequod* meets the one-armed captain of the *Samuel Enderby*.

> With his ivory arm frankly thrust forth in welcome, the other captain advanced, and Ahab, putting out his ivory leg, and crossing the ivory arm (like two sword-fish blades) cried out. . . . "Where did'st thou see the White Whale?—How long ago?"
>
> "The White Whale," said the Englishman, pointing his ivory arm towards the East, and taking a rueful sight along it, as if it had been a telescope; "There I saw him, on the Line, last season."
>
> "And he took that arm off, did he?" asked Ahab. . . .
>
> "Aye, he was the cause of it, at least; and that leg, too?"
> (100:437–38)

So does the one-armed captain repeat, more than eighty chapters later, the demonstrative gesture of Elijah; so does the mortal target (the death-carrying white whale) approach, successively aimed at by two indexes. And once again, the truth index is the prophetic and prosthetic default of the telescopic arm that, prior to vision, can blindly see from afar.

# Retroprospection

MAURICE BLANCHOT WRITES:

Prophecy is not just a future language. It is a dimension of language that engages it in relationships with time that are much more important than the simple discovery of certain events to come. To foresee and announce some future event does not amount to much, if this future takes place in the ordinary course of events and *finds expression in the regularity of language.* But prophetic speech announces an impossible future, or makes the future it announces, because it announces it, something impossible. . . . When speech becomes prophetic, it is not the future that is given, it is the present that is taken away, and with it any possibility of a firm, stable, lasting presence.[17]

The prophet only becomes a prophet after the fact, by a kind of returning stroke in which time stammers, carrying any stable present in a hurricane that turns and returns upon itself. History, as one says, stammers; whether it is so-called real history, as posted on the great program of the world, or fictive histories or stories, as narrated in short stories, novels, and other fictions (without mentioning the great stammering that could very well occur between the two).

To tell or to foretell, to read or to fore-read what is coming—this would be a kind of *retroprospection.* And it is the trace of this retroprospective movement that I am trying to follow in Melville, who has evoked it as such, most notably in *Pierre, or The Ambiguities,* according to the strange logic of an arriving motion that, if I dare say so, ebbs into the past to the very extent it surges toward the future.[18] At the beginning of book 3 ("The Presentiment and the Verification"), speaking of the "apparition" in the form of a face that has been haunting Pierre for some time, Melville writes in fact that "it had still beamed upon him; vaguely *historic and prophetic*; backward, hinting of some irrevocable sin; forward, pointing to some inevitable ill."[19] And it is again of this apparition or "shadow" of retroprospective reach that it is a question further on, when, rhetorically addressing "fathers and mothers all the world round," Melville warns of what must be called a movement of *retroreading*. Declining the future in the past, he writes:

> Thy little one may not now comprehend the meaning of those words and those signs, by which, in its innocent presence, thou thinkest to disguise the sinister thing ye would hint. Not now he knows; not very much even of the externals he consciously remarks; but if, in after-life [that is, in the beyond of a surviving to come], Fate puts the chemic key of the cipher into his hands; then how swiftly and how wonderfully, he reads all the obscurest and most obliterate inscriptions he finds in his memory; yea, and rummages himself all over, for still hidden writings to read. Oh, darkest lessons of Life have thus been read. (4:70)

Reading backward, reading against the grain—this would also be reading ahead.

# Deluge and Delirium

IN *ISRAEL POTTER*, Benjamin Franklin is described as an ageless patriarch. Living, as those biblical ones do, a great number of years, he seems to extend his life expectancy both forward and backward, according to a temporal elasticity tensely held between memory and anticipation.

> Yet though he was thus lively and vigorous to behold, spite of his seventy-two years (his exact date at the time) somehow, the incredible seniority of an antediluvian seemed his. Not the years of the calendar wholly, but also the years of sapience. His white hairs and mild brow, spoke of the future as well as the past. He seemed to be seven score years old; that is, three-score and ten of prescience added to three score and ten of remembrance, makes just seven score years in all. (*IP*, 7:39)

The antediluvian Benjamin Franklin—who seems gifted with the strange ability of *retro-aging*—meets or brushes against the silhouette of the diluvian Noah. Would the inventor of the lightning rod (of whom one could think that he is, if not the ancestor, at least the tutelary figure of all future traveling salesmen who specialize in lightning rods) have anything to do (or to see) with the first man called upon to protect himself from the first and greatest of all thunderstorms?

Melville eagerly invokes the flood, as well as Noah. He does so in some scattered notes, for example, whose deciphering is rendered difficult by the absence of context:

Eclipse

Noah after the Flood                              Cap.[tain] Pollard
                                                  of Nan. [tucket][20]


This "Captain Pollard, of Nantucket," is in fact mentioned in
*Moby-Dick* (chapter 45), his sunken ship being exemplary of the di-
sasters wrought by the sperm whale (45:206). As for the diluvian
figure of Noah, it appears on numerous occasions over the course of
the novel. Here it is, in chapter 58, where Ishmael admonishes his
future readers by calling upon them, "Yea, foolish mortals, Noah's
flood is not yet subsided; two thirds of the fair world it yet covers"
(58:273). Here it is again, when Ishmael explains that Ahab's whaling
ship, like others, has no need to touch land, since it transports enough
drinking water in its hold to sail on for years. In this manner, were
it reached by "the news that another flood had come," its sailors
would have no other answer than: "Well, boys, here's the ark!"
(87:382). Here it is, finally (for this is, if I am not mistaken, its last
occurrence) on the third day of the chase, when, before his final
confrontation with the white whale and only moments before his
death, Ahab gazes at the sea and, otherwise almost stammering, cries
out: "An old, old sight, and yet somehow so young. . . . The same!—
the same!—the same to Noah as to me" (135:565).

Among all these evocations of the flood, there is one in particular
upon which I believe I should linger for a while, since it addresses
itself to the reader (that I am and follow [*que je suis*]). And perhaps it
even enunciates, doing so at least allusively, something about reading.

In *Moby-Dick*, then, in a chapter on "The Fossil Whale," Ishmael
seems to think it necessary to "remind the reader" that there exists
an apparent genealogical continuity between antediluvian whales
and the whales of today:

> While in the earlier geological strata there are found the fossils
> of monsters now almost completely extinct; the subsequent relics
> discovered in what are called the Tertiary formations seem the
> connecting, or at any rate intercepted links, between the antechron-
> ical creatures, and those whose remote posterity are said to have
> entered the Ark; all the Fossil Whales hitherto discovered belong

to the Tertiary period, which is the last preceding the superficial formations. And though none of them precisely answer to any known species of the present time, they are yet sufficiently akin to them in general respects, to justify their taking rank as Cetacean fossils. (104:456)

Thus, in the great archive of the world, the whale is a document, a trace, a line of writing that makes possible the drawing of a thread going back from today all the way to the flood and even prior to that, prior to time itself. While meditating upon the Leviathan skeletons, skulls, and vertebrae, Ishmael reads them; he hands them over to a reading, like a chronicle diving into the depths of the ante- (or the anti-) chronical. Thus, dreaming of archeocetology, Ishmael describes himself: "I am, by a flood, borne back to that wondrous period, ere time itself can be said to have begun" (104:457).

This flow, flood, or deluge that carries the narrator is not that of Noah's Ark. It is not the same as the one that carries the patriarch and his ark. It would, rather, be a kind of *antediluvian flood*, one not surging through the course of world history and following the linear and chronological flow of its events but occurring instead on an anamnesic—and anachronistic—line.

Two floods are therefore crossing here, which must be distinguished.

The first one is the biblical and patriarchal one, which engages Noah in a project of salvation concerning a pair of every creature, in order to keep in reserve a sample of the world that would deliver it to the flow of ulterior history.

The other carries Ishmael off, making him dream of going back in time. It is, by contrast, a flood and a deluge that has more to do with a kind of delirium (*delirare* means "to come out of the furrow," out of the *lira*, the drawn line). It is a *lire*—a reading—that goes against the tide, therefore, that cuts across traces and strata, and, failing to find ties and continuous connections, it follows intermittent links—"intercepted links," as Ishmael puts it (104:456).

Listen to him in his *délire*, his reading-undoing delirium: "I look round to shake hands with Shem. I am horror-struck at this antemosaic, unsourced existence of the unspeakable terrors of the whale, which, having been before all time, must needs exist after all humane ages are over" (104:457).

At the very moment in which he jointly speaks of the very beginning and the very end, everything occurs, therefore, as if Ishmael were implicitly opposing two movements—that are also two types—of reading.

On one side—Noah's side—there is continuity (what Blanchot calls "the regularity of language" and "the ordinary course of events"). It is an uninterrupted groove or furrow that follows the direction of descent and of consequence: by preserving a sample of each species, Noah will have saved the continuity of the world that, in the flow of the flood, runs downstream of itself.

On the other side—the side of Ishmael's anachronistic reading—there is a madly undone, reading-undoing furrow that goes backward in time, rambling and straying, skipping from link to link, without an actual chain ever holding it.

What is clear is that, after the flood during which Noah stores away pieces of the world in order to deliver them unto postdiluvian posterity, nothing will happen but the unfolding of a program already archived in the Ark. But with Ishmael's antediluvian delirium, who can tell what sails against the tide and toward the antechronical? Who can tell what it is that will surge unexpected?

To read in this fashion immemorial Genesis, from the *retroprospection* of a 1851 novel, is evidently to let oneself be carried off by a flow or a deluge similar to the one described by Ishmael when he abandons himself to his archeocetological dreams. What takes place then is first and foremost an *appareillage* of reading.

Yes, an *appareillage*, in both possible senses of that French term, which are not foreign to each other in this context: (1) the disposition of an apparel, apparatus, or accessory, in short, of *prostheses* toward a certain usage (the way one speaks of an electrical apparatus or else, in medicine, of the equipment, *appareillage*, of the hearing-impaired); (2) the casting off and departure of a vessel, leaving its docks and moorings, raising the anchor as it *appareille*, that is to say, sails off, precisely.

It is Ahab who, in *Moby-Dick*, incarnates this *appareillage*. It is he who, with his mutilated body, equipped or *appareillé* with a prosthesis, calls for a kind of unanchoring of reading in order for it to rise in the winds of prophecy, for untying it—to paraphrase Father Mapple—from the connecting strands and mighty cables that ensure, indeed, anchor it to a safe haven. Ahab is the prophetic reader. He is the one who promises prophecy even before he can see clearly, whereas Noah shows nothing but foresight.[21]

# Leaks (Over and Beyond the Archive)

COME, FOLLOW WITH ME, to see without foresight the figures of Ahab as allegory of the reader. You will see him reading as a navigator at risk, threatened with shipwreck—this Ahab who takes after prophets and grammarian interpreters, as Quintus was suggesting.

Look. Ahab's vessel, the *Pequod*, is weighted with a charge, a shipment that balances it as it sails the deep seas. This weight, this ballast or load, transforms it into a reading head that, sailing across the most raging of waters, seems erect nonetheless, constantly rising toward its heading at the horizon. In chapter 110 of *Moby-Dick*, one fully discovers the ballast that weighs and thus stabilizes the ship. Searching for a leak in the barrels of oil piled up in the hold, the crew of the Pequod digs deep into the most profound layers of this floating geology.

> Upon searching, it was found that the casks last struck into the hold were perfectly sound, and the leak must be further off. So, it being calm weather, they broke out deeper and deeper, disturbing the slumbers of the huge ground-tier butts; and from that black midnight sending those gigantic moles into the daylight above. So deep did they go; and so ancient, and corroded, and weedy the aspect of the lowermost puncheons, that you almost looked next for some mouldy cornerstone cask containing coins of Captain Noah, with copies of the posted placards, vainly warning the infatuated old world from the flood. (110:476)

These antediluvian placards that the digging sailors appear to bring to light, these fictitious archiplacards that have remained at the bottom of the hold since Noah's Ark, recall the great poster of the world program posted in chapter 1 of *Moby-Dick*. Upon it, there figured Ishmael's voyage, framed and enclosed between an uncertain American election and a bloody Afghan war. In both cases, for there to be an announcement (that is to say, a kind of prophecy, whether or not it takes place, *in fine*), for some event to be predicted or foreseen as coming while having already left traces of this coming, there must occur a kind of safekeeping, the setting up of an enclosure, of which the bottom of the hold offers a gripping image. Prophetic reading presupposes that traces have been left, in one way or another, that these traces have been subjected to a stratified burial in a kind of crypt where broad daylight has suddenly penetrated.

But this is only one of the necessary conditions, and not a sufficient one. For the prophetic dimension of reading is not uniquely, not simply of the order of a mere archaeological excavation, which unearths buried layers.

Go figure what would be the sufficient conditions to produce a prophecy—not to mention its eventual realization . . . What I think I can say, minimally, following Ishmael, is that over and above the exhumation of antediluvian archives one would need a kind of storm—a wind or thunderstorm, a hurricane or a cyclone—*in the act of their reading*. In order for the unexpected to surge over and out of the crypt already found there, what would be needed—you must have a foreboding sense of it—for prophetic deciphering is that it be carried off by a flow coming from the future. In short, one would have to be able to *read* [lire] Noah's placards according to the kind of undoing (a delirium and an undoing of reading, a *délire*) that had gripped Ishmael in his own wavering ascent (or descent) toward ante- or anti-chronic whales.

In his narrative of the exhumation scene that occupies us here, Ishmael is, after all, feigning his fear of what he must be, at bottom, awaiting: "Well was it that the Typhoons did not visit them then," he says, speaking of the moment at which the archives are vulnerably exposed on the deck, having barely ascended from the hull where they were sleeping. "Top-heavy was the ship," he adds, as heavy with potential readings "as a dinnerless student with all Aristotle in his head" (110:476). But for reading to be something other than an exercise in the stacked-up accumulation of archives, something other than an archivistics, of which Noah's Ark is the provident figure, one would still need the storm, whose hour has yet to come. One would need the ills still to come, which the event of reading awaits for its advent.

This, at least, is what Ahab seems to know without knowing, he who expected nothing—no event worthy of that name—from the speleological search after an oil leak in the barrels. In the preceding chapter, when Starbuck, the chief mate, comes to inform him that "the oil in the hold is leaking" and that it might be necessary to "up Burtons and break out," Ahab (it is no coincidence) was busy *writing*, he was "tracing his old courses again" upon "a general chart of the oriental archipelagoes spread before him" (109:473). At first, Ahab refuses to order the archeological digging aimed at repairing the leak. Not only does he fail to see the necessity of it, in fact, he even proceeds to orate *in praise of leaks*: "Heave-to here for a week to tinker a parcel of old hoops? . . . Let it leak! I'm all aleak myself. Aye! Leaks in leaks! Not only full of leaky casks, but those leaky casks are in a leaky ship; and that's a far worse plight than the Pequod's, man. Yet I don't stop to plug my leak; for who can find it in the deep-loaded hull; or how hope to plug it, even if found, in this life's howling gale?" (109:474).

It is only against his will, as if it were a waste of time, that Ahab finally agrees to the search in the hold. But it is clear that, so far as he is concerned, nothing will emerge from an operation that, essentially, has everything to do with care and foresight, with archivistics and the filling of breaches. In relation to the concern for plugging, filling, or preserving that animates his chief mate, Ahab incarnates ruptures, stabs, and punctures. Ahab is nothing but this moment, recurring throughout the novel, in which all the envelopes shatter and all the lines break. They break down and leak. These ruptures, which come to him from the *no heading* of his mad navigation toward that which comes, constitute the condition, the *other* condition for the prophetic and prosthetic advent of the event of reading.

This condition comes from over and beyond the hull [*outre-cale*], from over and beyond the grave, over and beyond the crypt. It comes from over and beyond the ark, over and beyond the skins [*outre les outres*] in which are stored the fossil remainders, beyond the beyond itself [*outre l'outre même*] of a surviving that ensures the crossing of the flood and of the times of the storm—the enclosure must burst. There must flow, rich with fear, a *blood of ink*.[22]

# "Leviathan is the text,"
## or Generalized Meteorism

JONAH, WHOM *Moby-Dick* invokes on numerous occasions, is in many respects a figure parallel to Noah.[1] This time, by contrast to the situation during the flood (but always in the middle of a storm), it is not a human being, in fact, it is not Noah who encloses in his box the coupled specimen of each animal species. It is, on the contrary, a beast—and what a beast!—that swallows a human: "And Jonah was in the belly of the fish three days and three nights" (Jon. 1:17).

The monstrous beast is not, in Jonah, a sample of world that the world keeps in order to survive, as the animal pairs are for Noah. The beast is here alone. It enters into a ménage with no other. It is immense and, one easily imagines, squalid [*immonde*]. The beast, here, is the other, the wholly other. It is the inhuman, the ahuman, or the superhuman, from the heart of which Jonah will nonetheless ascend toward the fortress of his God, along with the prayer that rises. And Jonah will finally find himself standing on solid ground.

> The waters closed in over me; the deep surrounded me; weeds were wrapped around my head at the roots of the mountains. I went down to the land whose bars closed upon me forever; yet you *brought up my life from the Pit*, O Lord my God. As my life was ebbing away, I remembered the Lord; and my prayer came to you, into your holy temple. . . . Then the Lord spoke to the fish, and it spewed Jonah out upon the dry land. (Jon. 2:5–10)

The whale is a fortress—that, at least, is what Ishmael explicitly says in *Moby-Dick*: "I know a man that, in his lifetime, has taken three hundred and fifty whales. I account that man more honorable than that great captain of antiquity who boasted of taking as many walled towns" (24:111).

But what the narrator of the novel constantly affirms and reaffirms is that the whale is a book. Or rather, as the book of *Moby-Dick* is written under the quill of Ishmael, its scribing narrator, so the whale *becomes* equally a book.

Early on in the novel, in a chapter dedicated to Ahab *reading* and *inscribing* his maps (chapter 44), the whale is also described as *tracing lines*. Look at both of them, then, as they read and write, each in his turn.

First Ahab, alone:

> Had you followed Captain Ahab down into his cabin . . . you would have seen him go to a locker in the transom, and bringing out a large wrinkled roll of yellowish sea charts, spread them before him on his screwed-down table. Then seating himself before it, you would have seen him intently study the various lines and shadings which there met his eyes; and with slow but steady pencil trace additional courses over spaces that before were blank. At intervals, he would refer to piles of old log-books beside him, wherein were set down the seasons and places in which, on various former voyages of various ships, sperm whales had been captured or seen. (44:198)

Ahab recalls Jonah here, reading and writing in his cabin, lit by a "heavy pewter lamp suspended in chains over his head, continually rocked with the motion of the ship." But Ahab himself becomes a kind of page, a bearer of signs, "his wrinkled brow" (akin to the "wrinkled roll" of the previous paragraph) becoming the substrate and support upon which are projected "shifting gleams and shadows of lines." It is almost as if, pursues Ishmael, "while he himself was marking out lines and courses on the wrinkled charts, some invisible pencil was also tracing lines and courses upon the deeply marked chart of his forehead" (ibid.). It is "almost every night" that Ahab writes so, and that he is so written. Ahab constantly writes and rewrites, "almost every night some pencil marks were effaced and others were substituted." Night after night, Ahab retraces the trails of the whales, which are themselves lines as well.

And here now—look—leviathans are writing in their turn: "The sperm whales, guided by some infallible instinct—say, rather, secret intelligence from the Deity—mostly swim in *veins*, as they are called; continuing their way along a given ocean-line." (44:199)

As it traces the divine lines that others, such as Ahab, will endeavor to decipher with the help of divinatory tracings, the sperm whale is also covered with traces, with marks of all kinds, akin to a kind of ancient book. In a later chapter dedicated to the "blanket" of the whale, that is, to its "skin," Ishmael thus describes Leviathan on the verge of becoming-text.

> In life, the visible surface of the Sperm Whale is not the least among the many marvels he presents. Almost invariably it is all over obliquely crossed and re-crossed with numberless straight marks in thick array, something like those in the finest Italian line engravings. . . . Nor is this all. In some instances, to the quick, observant eye, those linear marks, as in a veritable engraving, but afford the ground for far other delineations. These are hieroglyphical; that is, if you call those mysterious ciphers on the walls of pyramids hieroglyphics, then that is the proper word to use in the present connection. (68:306)

Elsewhere, it is the forehead of the whale that calls for a physiognomic deciphering, one for which Ishmael confesses his inability. He then turns to the reader of the novel being written and calls upon this reader to *read*, that is, to decipher and translate an unknown language: "How may unlettered Ishmael hope to read the awful Chaldee of the Sperm Whale's brow? I but put that brow before you. Read it if you can" (79:347)

These marks carried by the whale "as if they were engraved upon the body itself" (68:306), this living writ traced to the quick—these are not only the result of Ahab's own writing (he who inscribes endlessly rewritten courses upon his charts and is himself marked with lines upon his brow). They are also Ishmael's, the scribing narrator, who makes or lets be engraved upon his own body *memoranda* competing with the very work he is in the process of writing:

The skeleton dimensions I shall now proceed to set down [the following chapter is indeed entitled "Measurements of the Whale's Skeleton"] are copied verbatim from my right arm, where I had them tattooed; as in my wild wanderings at that period, there was no other secure way of preserving such valuable statistics. But as I was crowded for space, and wished the other parts of my body to remain a blank page for the poem I was then composing—at least, what untattooed parts might remain—I did not trouble myself with the odd inches; nor indeed, should inches at all enter into a congenial admeasurement of the whale. (102:451)

This "poem" that Ishmael is composing under our eyes, could it be *Moby-Dick*? Could it be what I am reading to you at this very moment? It does seem that Ishmael's body, the body of the scribing narrator, is itself thereby becoming the implicit substrate of what his reader will read (what he already reads). As with every notebook, this body is the object of an economic calculation regarding its mnemonic usage. This living body is a prosthesis of memory, to which one confines dead signs. It is a body on the verge of becoming prosthetic, amputable, like a page from a notebook that one might tear out in order to insert and inscribe it in a work to come.

I catch my breath for an instant and, in order not to forget, I throw a glance backward, upon the trail freshly traced by my readings.

The whale, I was saying, writes. It *is* writing. Ahab too is writing. He rewrites the whale and its trails, much as he becomes a kind of wrinkled parchment. Ishmael, finally, writes: he collects the various traces of writing—the lines, the folds, the wrinkles, the marks, the tracings, the trails and the fossils . . .—he offers them to a reading to the extent that he incorporates them to himself, becoming a kind of whale book destined to be carved up.

In another chapter, Ishmael will go so far as to imagine for himself a swollen body, overflowing itself in a kind of universal blister, becoming monstrous according to the measure of his monster-book:

From his mighty bulk the whale affords a most congenial theme whereon to enlarge, amplify, and generally expatiate. Would you,

you could not compress him. By good rights he should only be treated of in imperial folio. . . . But when Leviathan is the text, the case is altered. Fain am I to stagger to this emprise under the weightiest words of the dictionary. And here be it said, that whenever it has been convenient to consult one in the course of these dissertations, I have invariably used a huge quarto edition. . . . One often hears of writers that rise and swell with their subject, though it may seem but an ordinary one. How, then, with me, writing of this Leviathan? Unconsciously my chirography expands into placard capitals. Give me a condor's quill! Give me Vesuvius' crater for an inkstand! (104:455–56)

In short, he who writes can no longer hold or contain himself. He who carries within him this whale book on the whale, he for whom "Leviathan is the text" (weakly translated into French as "Leviathan serves as the theme"), he becomes *a whale author* (and not, as the French has it, "a whaling author").

*Leviathan is the text*—this means, no doubt, that the book, this very book (*Moby-Dick*) is written *on* the whale, as a subject or a theme. But equally leviathanic is the text to the extent that, like the whale, it encloses and contains all. It welcomes all: it is a world in the world. It takes after the myth of the Ark in the flood and that of Jonah, enclosing both within itself.

Ishmael, who carries within and upon himself, within and upon his very skin, the book to come—Ishmael is also contained within it. And the "placard capitals" of his graphology, which are like the sign or symptom of this double and monstrous reciprocal enclosure, also evoke those of chapter 1: this "placard" or "bill" on which was posted, already in capital letters, "a sort of brief interlude and solo between more extensive performances," in "the grand programme of Providence" (1:7). In addition, in its exorbitant content, Ishmael's text would already be like a magisterial amplification of "The Lightning-Rod Man": the "I," the narrator is here the center (the focus and the hearth), who produces and contains everything yet, like a Jonah, also risks being engulfed in another center, the monstrous center of the other, which he has made surge. It is as if he who says "I," whether he is called Ishmael or whether he remains the anonymous narrator receiving the visit of a stranger selling lightning rods, as if this I was producing a monster-providence, a prevision that shows everything—even that which is occurring to us, his readers—ultimately to end by engulfing everything: me, you, and he who narrates.

Thus, this leviathanic text would be prosthetic and prophetic at once, since it is written by a scribing narrator who would wish to be as great as the subject he has in him (or that has him in it). In this dilatation that touches writing and reading, this hypertrophy in which one does not know who contains what and what contains whom, in short, in the movement of self-swelling that could be described as a *generalized meteorism of the text*, there are indeed found the conditions of its prostheticity (of its artificial dismemberment by bursting or explosion, by rupture of the organic envelop that contains it) and of its propheticity (the inflation of sense overflowing toward an outside to come).

The text is, in a word, *swollen*. It is distended to the point of rupture.[2] It is on the verge of bursting, bloated by its own daring, impertinent, and untenable tenor. Such a text, as artificial as a supplement that would not cease growing against nature, calls for a prosthetic and prophetic reading.

But wait. What is Ahab doing? What does the one holding the helm like a grammarian of the sea do when he punctures and kills the whale? What is this textual being, who (like everybody, like the *entire world*) inhabits the novel, doing? And what is he doing when he pierces the envelope of a Leviathan, which one now has the right to suspect is the very text?

"Ahab's harpoon had shed older blood than the Pharaohs'. Methuselah seems a schoolboy," says Ishmael at one point (104:457). Ahab and his own point, Ahab and his engraving awl, Ahab and his *style*— Ahab, then, does sail on the same seas as Noah and his Ark. But he does not manage so well the archived menagerie of the world. In addition, he cuts into its largest sample—Leviathan—in order to make flow an anachronistic blood.

In short, one could think that Ahab does nothing with his harpoon but pierce and puncture the walls of that other crypt in the form of an ark that a whale is. As for the whale, it is quite capable of archiving by engulfing at least a Jonah and many other samples that are not far from making up a rest of the world. But precisely, as much as Noah incarnates the cumulative archivistics of the ark, so does Ahab, when he opens and punctures with his style the reserve of the whale, when he lets surge a source that defies the linear continuity of the time of reading. It is surely not a coincidence that the whale—this sort of complement or supplement of ark—seems to be the only one to have escaped the archiving protection of Noah, as Ishmael himself notes: "In Noah's flood he despised Noah's Ark; and if ever the world is to be again flooded . . . then the eternal whale will still survive, and rearing upon the topmost crest of the equatorial flood, spout his frothed defiance to the skies" (105:462).

If Noah is the man of archived memory who enables prevision as the economic calculation of the future, if Noah is a kind of great meteorologist, then Ahab is a storm-man. The meteoric "Old Thunder" is himself an interruption. Or rather, an interception: what he captures is precisely what has escaped the archive of the ark. It is the *anarchive*, in which, in a retreat without reserve, both the event and its prophecy to come are lying in wait.

Moreover, the outrageous Captain Ahab, who is enclosed in the text of the novel he inhabits, dreams of piercing the walls that lock him in. He wants to burst the envelop of this Leviathan-text that circles his horizon, without knowing what he will find on the other side. And to his chief mate, Starbuck, who wishes to stop him in his mad hunt for the sperm whale, Ahab does in fact answer: "How can the prisoner reach outside except by thrusting through the wall? To me, the white whale is that wall, shoved near to me. Sometimes I think there's naught beyond. But 'tis enough" (36:164).

To pierce the wall of the whale-text, therefore, may not be to escape or exit the text, which may very well not have a beyond or an outside. There is no hors-text, Ahab seems to suspect at the very moment he cries out that he wants to get out of it.

And then what? You ask.

Then, the outside of a text is, no doubt, still inside, according to the structure of mutual enclosures that has not ceased to pursue us since I have begun reading for you. Besides, it is because the hors-text is still part of the text that one can decipher in it, retropropheti-cally, the announcement of something that the text could not have literally wanted to say (or predict).

Still, even if the text does contain, in a certain manner, its own outside within, this is not to say that it partakes of a continuous topography. The enclosure does not operate without walls, without fortresses, without crypts and vaults, without faults and fissures, and without abysses, too. In short, if it does blur the simple logic of bor-ders (an alternative on each side, hither and thither), the contiguous proliferation, the *limitrophy* of enclosures also multiplies in many respects the solutions of continuity. It increases the thresholds, the ruptures, and the interruptions. It cultivates and feeds them, strengthens them—all on the inside of the text, there where prophecy surges in the self-tearing of its weave.

The propheticity of the text—or, if you prefer, its prophecies of prophecies—is also its *self-interruption*.

# The Fire, the Bonds

LIKE THE LIGHTNING-ROD MAN, like the salesman of lightning rods who bursts in on the narrator of that short story, Ahab, "Old Thunder" Ahab, also handles strange metallic sticks that capture lightning, as can be seen most notably in the chapter entitled "The Candles." There, Ishmael describes the lightning rods of Ahab's vessel, meticulously comparing the usage of those made for land and those for sea: "Now, as the lightning rod to a spire on shore is intended to carry off the perilous fluid into the soil; so the kindred rod which at sea some ships carry to each mast, is intended to conduct it into the water. . . . But . . . the lower parts of a ship's lightning-rods . . . are generally made in long slender links" (119:505).

Terrorized by flashes of lightning during the storm that has just burst (the *Pequod*, writes Ishmael, "was torn of her canvas, and bare-poled was left to fight a Typhoon which had struck her directly ahead"; 119:503), Starbuck, the chief mate, orders that the lightning rods of the ship be readied. But, suddenly emerging from the darkness as "sky and sea roared and split with the thunder," his staggering way lit by "elbowed lances of fire," Ahab comes forward and cries: "Avast!"

Ahab thus *interrupts* the chain or the ties of a relay that, from link to link, could have led the striking meteoric energy and diverted it toward the water. Immediately, a kind of miracle occurs. Just as Ahab contradicts the order of his chief mate, the latter is heard crying twice: "Look aloft! . . . The corpusants! The corpusants!" (119:505). Addressing himself directly, without relay, to the "clear

48

spirit of clear fire" (119:507), Starbuck says, after the manner of Shakespeare's Lear, "the lightning flashes through my skull; mine eye-balls ache and ache." Ahab the interrupter, Ahab the disjunctive breaker, himself burns with the meteoric fire he has seized and captured. And this fire appears to radiate, to communicate at a distance from his prosthetic, one-legged body to the other extension of himself that is his harpoon. The spear he will throw into the whale, the iron forged in fire that already points its arrow toward the future of a mortal hunt, can be seen emerging, firing, *ahead and at the head* of Ahab's whaleboat: "Ahab's harpoon . . . remained firmly lashed . . . so that it projected beyond his whale-boat's bow; but the sea . . . had caused the loose leather sheath to drop off; and from the keen steel barb there now came a leveled flame of pale, forked fire" (119:508).

In this forked flame, Starbuck, the chief mate with foresight, reads a bad omen and tries to reverse the course of the navigation. But Ahab stops him again, interrupts the flame and the augural reading it provokes.

As the silent harpoon burned there like a serpent's tongue, Starbuck grasped Ahab by the arm—"God, God is against thee, old man; forbear! 'tis an ill voyage! ill begun, ill continued; let me square the yards, while we may, old man, and make a fair wind of it homewards, to go on a better voyage than this."

Overhearing Starbuck, the panic-stricken crew instantly ran to the braces—though not a sail was left aloft. . . . But dashing the rattling lightning links to the deck, and snatching the burning harpoon, Ahab waived it like a torch among them; swearing to transfix with it the first sailor that but cast loose a rope's end. Petrified by his aspect, and still more shrinking from the fiery dart that he held, the men fell back in dismay and Ahab again spoke:—

"All your oaths to hunt the White Whale are as *binding* as mine; and heart, soul, and body, lungs and life, old Ahab is *bound*. And that ye may know to what tune this heart beats: look ye here; thus I blow out the last fear!" And with one blast of his breath he extinguished the flame.

As in the hurricane that sweeps the plain, men fly the neighborhood of some lone, gigantic elm, whose very height and strength bur render it so much the more unsafe, because so much the more a mark for thunderbolts; so at those last words of Ahab's many of the mariners did run from him in a terror of dismay. (119:508; emphasis added)

Ahab's repeated interruptions, his breaking of chains, ties, and relays, and, finally, his cutting short every possibility of return—these are ultimately turned around and reversed into a binding, into an attachment and a far superior chain: not only does he remind the crew of the sworn covenant that binds them, but he also offers his own body as an example, his proper body as the very figure of the organic bond.

Strange, don't you think, for someone whose own leg hangs only by a thread? This rupture of organicity unleashed by the prosthetic captain—could it be the promise of a transmutation into a new body, one more organic still? His prophecy would then be the absolute bond, the absolute *hold* on a body—organic and perhaps politic— solidly intertwined in the threads of a bond that commits him.

To believe this would be to trust, it would be to rely on a reading still all too linear (that is to say, all too organic, precisely) of the immense texture or contexture that is the Leviathan-text, of which Ahab partakes while tearing it apart. It would be to forget that the rupture of lines and of chains incarnated by this great disjunctive breaker is, first of all, an unceasing *self-interruption* of the Leviathan-text. The great body, whose cloth contains and envelops other bodies, could not *form one body* [faire corps] for long: its monstrous greatness, which renders it prosthetic and prophetic, destines it to a self-tearing.

# Lost at Sea [*Déboussolé*]

IN FACT, as the end of the novel approaches, the figures of interruption are multiplied, as are the reversals, the inversions of sense. In short, the lines of navigation and destination that have borne the characters until now are beginning to lose their orientation, their magnetic pole, their arrow. They are losing the North, like the needle of the *Pequod*'s compass, disoriented by the lightning that has struck it: "The two compasses pointed East and the Pequod was as infallibly going West . . . eyeing the transpointed compasses, the old man, with the sharp of his extended hand, now took the precise bearing of the sun, and satisfied that the needles were exactly inverted, shouted out his orders for the ship's course to be changed accordingly" (124:517).

Like a disoriented reader—or else, to return to Quintus's metaphor, like a grammarian oracle navigating without heading and drifting toward shipwreck—Ahab will go so far as to make, out of his own hands, a new compass of fortune, which will indicate the new course to follow: "my men"—he announces proudly to his crew, speaking of himself in the third person, as if of another—"my men, the thunder turned old Ahab's needles; but out of this bit of steel Ahab can make one of his own, that point as true as any" (124:518).

Yet, as Ishmael makes clear in the penultimate chapter before the Epilogue, the great magnet of the Leviathan-text, the pole that magnetizes its crossing, is the whale itself. It is in its trail that the "future wake" of the Leviathan-text forging ahead through the darkness is readable in advance.

For such is the wonderful skill, prescience of experience, and invincible confidence acquired by some great natural geniuses among the Nantucket commanders; that from the simple observation of a whale when last descried, they will, under certain given circumstances, pretty accurately foretell both the direction in which he will continue to swim for a time, *while out of sight*, as well as his probable rate of progression during that period . . . for after being chased, and *diligently marked*, through several hours of daylight, then, when night obscures the fish, the creature's future wake through the darkness is almost as established to the sagacious mind of the hunter, as the pilot's coast is to him. So that to this hunter's wondrous skill, the proverbial evanescence of *a thing writ in water*, a wake, is to all desired purposes well nigh as reliable as the steadfast land. (134:555–56)

In a general fashion, the image of a wake to come is indeed propitious to evoke that of the advance upon oneself, which carries and carries off every reader in his expectations. But in *this* book, which tells of the pursuit of the white whale, in *this* tale, whose unique and obsessive object is the tracking of the sperm whale by the grammarian captain, then reading would have to merge entirely with the wake left by Moby Dick. Moby Dick or *Moby-Dick*: both the whale and the book to which it gives its name. To read *Moby-Dick*, to read its lines while reading the wake of Moby Dick in the book—as I am doing for you, in order to try to hold you back, you who forge ahead in the night of the future—would simply be to *pre-read* the Leviathan-text. For it is in the whale-text entitled *Moby-Dick*, it is *within the text itself* that the Leviathan-text is prescribed or preinscribed, as if by its very own point.

# The Laws of Fishing and of Reading

IN ITS PROPHETIC advance upon itself, the whale-text seems to attach itself to its own wake. The "great fish" seems to pull behind him a monster-text—a text within which it yet swims—anchored in him by some harpoon and its line. Thus, the laws of reading will resemble, for Ishmael, the laws of fishing.

In the chapter entitled "Fast-Fish and Loose-Fish," Ishmael seems to propose to give "an account of the laws and regulations of the whale fishery" (but you will see that it is in fact about us readers), laws of which a certain object named *waif* is "the grand symbol and badge" (89:395).

What, then, is the waif? Ishmael has explained it in an earlier chapter: it is a sharp iron pole equipped with a flag and jammed in the floating corpse of a dead whale "to mark its place in the sea." It is a "token of prior possession, should the boats of any other ship draw near" (87:390).

But what is this sign of belonging itself a "mark" and a "great symbol" of? Well, of a legislative "system," of which Ishmael extols, perhaps not without some irony, the "terse comprehensiveness" (89:395). This "system" is in fact contained in two phrases, in two sentences:

"I. A Fast-Fish belongs to the party fast to it ["party" being a juridical, technical term referring to the sides involved].

II. A Loose-Fish is fair game for anybody who can soonest catch it" (89:396).

The very brevity of this "masterly code" is not without inconveniences, adds Ishmael, since it "necessitates a vast volume of commentaries to expound it." And Ishmael submits to this necessity without delay, in the next paragraph. "What is a Fast-Fish?" he asks, adopting in his answer the tone of a jurist: "Alive or dead a fish is technically fast, when it is connected with an occupied ship or boat, by any medium at all controllable by the occupant or occupants,—a mast, an oar, a nine-inch cable, a telegraph wire, or a strand of cobweb, it is all the same. Likewise a fish is technically fast when it bears a waif, or any other recognized symbol of possession."

The allusion to the "vast volume" of technical "commentaries" explaining the "code" presumed to be masterfully brief cannot fail to evoke the entire book, *Moby-Dick*, that is to say, the Leviathan-text. And, in fact, Ishmael's ulterior reflections lead one to understand that, once again, the glosses made necessary by the code might very well expand and inflate, swell to leviathanic dimensions in a world-text.

> These two laws touching Fast-Fish and Loose-Fish, I say, will, on reflection, be found the fundamentals of all human jurisprudence. . . . But if the doctrine of Fast-Fish be pretty generally applicable, the kindred doctrine of Loose-Fish is still more widely so. That is internationally and universally applicable. What was America in 1492 but a Loose-Fish, in which Columbus struck the Spanish standard by way of waifing it for his royal master and mistress? . . . What India to England? What at last will Mexico be to the United States? All Loose-Fish.
>
> What are the Rights of Man and the Liberties of the World but Loose-Fish? What all men's minds and opinions but Loose-Fish? What is the great globe itself but a Loose-Fish? And what are you, reader, but a Loose-Fish and a Fast-Fish, too? (89:397–98)

Why did Jean Giono, the French translator, leave out this last sentence? Was he afraid, as translator, to be caught within the net of this binary code? Strange, at any rate, that at the very moment the text evokes the ties binding the reader to its own leviathanic body, this privileged reader that is the translator would choose to cut loose.

Be that as it may, then, the reader is both attached and detached. Swimming like a fish in the work, he is at once free—he belongs to no one—and anchored in the written body. The book owns the reader while losing him endlessly. For the reader—the Scheherazade that I am and follow, for example—is sent only as a detachment in order to attach himself to the text as much as possible, attaching himself to the task of detaching himself, expressing his attachment to what, of the text, escapes the text.

At bottom, would not the question be knowing to which category of fish belongs the Leviathan-text itself? That is to say: *Does the text attach itself or does it detach itself, of and from itself, by itself?* Put otherwise: when all threads, ropes, cables, and telegraph wires, of which Ishmael speaks "technically," when all these break, along with the bonds of all kind that sustain it, does the text lose its self-possession? Does it become mad? Or visionary? Or prophetic?

# In Detachment (Dis-Contraction)

ANOTHER STORY OF undone and detached bond is at the origin of the madness of poor Pip, the little black man whom Ishmael describes as a kind of prosthetic self-extension of Ahab. The latter does entertain with Pip a strange bond of resemblance and twin kinship. Ahab thus says to Pip: "Thou touchest my inmost centre, boy; thou art tied to me by cords woven of my heart-strings" (125:522). Whereas Pip declares to the captain: "Ye have not a whole body, sir; doe ye but use poor me for your one lost leg; only tread upon me, sir; I ask no more, so I remain a part of ye" (129:534).

Pip's madness is told in a chapter entitled "The Castaway": "A most significant event befell the most insignificant of the Pequod's crew; an event most lamentable; and which *ended* in providing the sometimes madly merry and predestinated craft with a living and ever accompanying prophecy of whatever shattered sequel might prove her own" (93:411; emphasis added).

The event about to be narrated to us is, therefore, as if suspended in advance toward its import. It has ended—says Ishmael, using a past tense that has the force of a future anterior—it *will have* ended, when we ourselves have finished reading, by being a prophecy of the end. The event in question (or its reading) is therefore detached in advance from its context, from the contexture of the lines that anchor or attach it to the course of the narrative. It is sent off, faraway, toward the end, where it awaits us *in detachment*.

But what is it that happened, precisely? As Ishmael explains, some sailors on a whaling ship are meant to remain on board during the hunt. Particularly so when, like Pip, they may be "an unduly slender, clumsy or timorous wight" (ibid.). Pip therefore belongs to the group called "shipkeepers." Because of his fragile constitution, his failing physical condition, he was a kind of *attaché* to safekeeping.

Yet one day one of the oarsmen in Stubb's (the second mate's) boat injures his hand. Pip is thus "put into his place."

The boat paddled upon the whale; and as the fish received the darted iron, it gave its customary rap, which happened, in this instance, to be right under poor Pip's seat. The involuntary consternation of the moment caused him to leap, paddle in hand, out of the boat; and in such a way, that part of the slack whale line coming against his chest, he breasted it overboard with him, so as to become entangled in it, when at last plumping into the water. That instant the stricken whale started on a fierce run, the line swiftly straightened; and presto! poor Pip came all foaming up to the chocks of the boat, remorselessly dragged there by the line, which had taken several turns around his chest and neck. (93:412)

Thus detached from the habitual function that bound him to the guard of the vessel, Pip, by accident, finds himself tragically moored to a line that, running at top speed, carries him to a certain death by strangulation. To the hunting sailors who ask themselves whether to cut the line, "Pip's blue, choked face" addressed this silent prayer: "Do, for God's sake!" (93:413). Stubb, the second mate, agrees to his request while cursing him ("Damn him, cut!") and this is how, by the rupture of the line and in one instant ("in a flash"), "the whale was lost and Pip was saved."

Frustrated, Stubb proceeds to teach a lesson to the poor survivor: "Stick to the boat, Pip," says he, pressing him to do everything to remain attached to the craft, were the occasion to repeat itself. For "we can't afford to lose whales" in this way, letting them become Loose-Fish. Yet after these chastising threats by the second mate, the scene does repeat itself, if with a difference.

But we are all in the hands of the gods; and Pip jumped again. It was under very similar circumstances to the first performance; but this time he did not breast out the line; and hence, when the whale started to run, Pip was left behind on the sea, like a hurried traveler's trunk. Alas! Stubb was but too true to his word. . . . Bobbing and down in that sea, Pip's ebon head showed like a head of cloves. . . . Stubb's inexorable back was turned upon him; and the whale was winged. In three minutes, a whole mile of shoreless ocean was between Pip and Stubb. . . . Now, in calm weather, to swim in the open ocean is as easy to the practiced swimmer as to ride in a spring-carriage ashore. But the awful lonesomeness is intolerable. The intense concentration of self in the middle of such a heartless immensity, my God! who can tell it? . . . Pip's ringed horizon began to expand around him miserably. (93:413–14)

Detached, this time, and in a terrifying manner, Pip nonetheless appears to be delivered to a contradictory movement. He is tossed about between a tightening and a loosening, between contraction and expansion, as if there were playing within him a terrible and simultaneous counterpoint of attachment and ultimate detachment.

I have already told you this, I believe: I have sometimes lived through a similar kinesthetic or polyaesthetic [cœnesthétique] experience. Sometimes, in fact, I close my eyes, lie down before sleeping or speaking while dreaming, and then my envelope seems to contract toward the infinitely small of the point, while inversely, the imaginary space that surrounds me is affected by an unceasing expansion toward the infinitely large. I have often thought that this sensation of exinvolution, as it were, that this horizontal and immobile vertigo was for me preceding while announcing the emergence of a voice deeply buried in the low register of my internal range.

For Pip, at any rate, the paradoxical experience of a contraction of the self, accompanied by a panoramic expansion in the same instant, which I would like to describe as one of dis-contraction, will have been the foreboding sign of his madness and of his prophetic vision.

By the merest chance the ship itself [i.e., the Pequod] at last rescued him; but from that hour the little negro went about the deck an idiot; such, at least, they said he was. The sea had jeeringly kept

his finite body up, but drowned the infinite of his soul. Not
drowned entirely, though. Rather carried down alive to wondrous
depths, where strange shapes of the unwarped primal world glided
to and fro before his passive eyes; and the miser-merman, Wisdom,
revealed his hoarded heaps. . . . He saw God's foot upon the treadle
of the loom, and spoke it; and therefore his shipmates called him
mad. So . . . wandering from all mortal reason, man comes at last
to that celestial thought, which, to reason, is absurd and frantic.
(93:414)

After having thus told the primal origin of Pip's visionary madness—to wit, his diving into a primal world—Ishmael proceeds to
end this troubling chapter by addressing the readers that we are, by
calling upon our clemency: "For the rest, blame not Stubb too hardly.
The thing is common in that fishery; and in the sequel of the narrative, it will then be seen what like abandonment befell myself"
(ibid.).

Let us not hold it against Stubb, he tells us, let our gaze go
through this insignificant character—so much more insignificant
than Pip, who gathers in his dive the signs of an immemorial past
and those of a future still remote. In short, let us detach ourselves
from him and from the piscatorial or economic context of the im-
mediate interests involved in the whale hunt. Let us attach ourselves instead to the prophetic content of the adventure *in and for
the book itself.* For it is not only a matter of Pip's prophetic faculty,
acquired during a brush with the great detachment that is death,
but also of Ishmael's prophecy about himself: his abandonment, in
the image of what has already happened to Pip. This is where Ishmael, here, cuts loose. He cuts the line that pulls our reading from
line to line. He interrupts the ties that bind him to the context and
sends us [*nous envoie*] in detachment, posting us directly to the end
of his tale: at the moment when, before the final point, he will find
himself alone, in the middle of the ocean. (We will come to it, I will
come back to it.)

Have the readers that we are, for all that, become prophets? Of
course not. I know nothing of the end, of the time of the end in

which prophecy will be verified. I have only a promise before my eyes, a prophecy of prophecy. Or, if you prefer, with everything I borrow from Ishmael the narrator, I still have nothing to offer you but a pure *form* of prophecy, without content. An empty envelope, as it were, sent toward the future of a tale, there where it awaits us.

# Return to Sender (The Dead Postman)

PROPHETIC READING thus implies a kind of return mail, in the image of the "returning-stroke" spoken of in "The Lightning-Rod Man," "when the earth, being overcharged with the fluid, flashes its surplus upward" (LRM, 122).

A bolt of lightning that, having fallen, goes back upward, a return to sender, in sum, as in the strange and uncanny postal scene in *Moby-Dick* entitled "The Jeroboam's Story." I address it to you, this scene, I entrust it to your reading; for it might well illuminate in return, by counterstroke, the retroprospective reading toward which I do not cease approaching, this reading retroprophetically magnetized toward a past that becomes future. The scene could speak to us, in sum, of this reading of which I would like to speak to you.

Here it is.

The *Pequod* has just encountered another ship, the *Jeroboam*, on board which there rages an epidemic. The two ships keep a safe distance, in respect of the quarantine regulations, but the two captains nonetheless communicate. The captain of the *Jeroboam*, a certain Mayhew, comes by in his boat, accompanied by a strange character named Gabriel, of which I will tell you more in a moment. There, tossed about by the waves, whose noise makes him miss some fragments of sentences, Mayhew answers Ahab's questions about the white whale. Suddenly, Ahab remembers that there is, in the *Pequod*'s letter-bag, a letter addressed to one of the *Jeroboam*'s officers. He sends Starbuck to fetch it.

Listen to Ishmael narrate the thing.

Every whale-ship takes out a goodly number of letters for various
ships, whose delivery to the persons to whom they may be addressed, depends upon the mere chance of encountering them in
the four oceans. Thus, most letters never reach their mark; and
many are only received after attaining an age of two or three years
or more.

Soon Starbuck returned with a letter in his hand. It was sorely
tumbled, damp, and covered with a dull, spotted, green mould, in
consequence of being kept in a dark locker of the cabin. Of such a
letter, Death himself might well have been the post-boy.

"Can'st not read it?" cried Ahab. "Give it me, man. Aye, aye,
it's but a dim scrawl. . . .

Ahab holding the letter, muttered: "Mr. Har—yes, Mr.
Harry—(a woman's pinny hand,—the man's wife, I'll wager)—
Aye—Mr. Harry Macey, Ship Jeroboam;—why it's Macey, and he's
dead!"

"Poor fellow! poor fellow! and from his wife," sighed Mayhew;
"but let me have it." (71:317–18)

The addressee of the letter, Harry Macey, was one of the chief
mates on the *Jeroboam*. He has, in fact, been dead for a long time: he
drowned when his vessel encountered Moby Dick, whom he relent-
lessly attacked in spite of the warnings of this singular member of
the crew, Gabriel.

For Gabriel—here we are—is described as a prophet. After the
fashion of Elijah, he is one of the prophetic figures that recur in
*Moby-Dick*. He wears a long coat of a "cabbalistic" cut and has "a
deep, settled, fanatic delirium" in his gaze. Let us read his tale, even
if it is that of a false prophet, a kind of impostor. For it does not
matter, at bottom. The moral of this fable, you will see, is that the
structure of prophecy, or of the prophecy of prophecy, wins over
those who, punctually, here and there, incarnate it. "His story was
this," says Ishmael. Listen:

He [Gabriel] had been originally nurtured among the crazy society
of Neskyeuna Shakers, where he had been a great prophet; in their
cracked, secret meetings, having several times descended from
heaven by the way of a trapdoor, announcing the speedy opening

of the seventh vial, which he carried in his vest-pocket. . . . A strange, apostolic whim having seized him, he had left Neskyeuna for Nantucket, where, with that cunning peculiar to craziness, he assumed a steady, common sense exterior, and offered himself as a green-hand candidate for the Jeroboam's whaling voyage. They engaged him; but straightaway upon the ship's getting out of sight of land . . . he announced himself as the archangel Gabriel, and commanded the captain to jump overboard. He published his manifesto, whereby he set himself forth as the deliverer of the isles of the sea and vicar-general of Oceanica. The unflinching earnestness with which he declared these things;—the dark, daring play of his sleepless, excited imagination . . . united to invest this Gabriel in the minds of the majority of the ignorant crew, with an atmosphere of sacredness. Moreover, they were afraid of him . . . the archangel cared little or nothing for the captain and mates; and since the epidemic had broken out, he carried a higher hand than ever; declaring that the plague, as he called it, was at his sole command. . . . The sailors, mostly poor devils, cringed and some of them fawned before him; in obedience to his instructions, sometimes rendering him personal homage, as to a god. Such things may seem incredible; but, however wondrous, they are true. Nor is the history of fanatics half so striking in respect to the measureless self-deception of the fanatic himself, as his measureless power of deceiving and bedeviling so many others. (71:314–15)

According to Ishmael, the intrinsic value (if there is any) of the prophet's prophecies therefore matters little. Everything lies in the effect of the prophecy, which, it is my hypothesis, receives its efficacy from what I am calling a promise or a prophecy of prophecy. But let me return to the premises of our postal scene.

Just prior to this scene, while responding to Ahab's questions, Captain Mayhew had endeavored to tell the story of Harry Macey, his deceased chief mate, and of his encounter with Moby Dick.

It seemed that the Jeroboam had not long left home, when upon speaking a whale-ship, her people were reliably apprised of the existence of Moby Dick, and the havoc he had made. Greedily sucking in this intelligence, Gabriel solemnly warned the captain against attacking the White Whale, in case the monster should be seen; in his gibbering insanity, pronouncing the White Whale to be no less a being than the Shaker God incarnated; the Shakers receiving the Bible. But when, some year or two afterwards, Moby Dick was fairly sighted from the mast-heads, Macey, the chief mate, burned with ardor to encounter him; and . . . despite all the archangel's denunciations and forewarnings, Macey. . . . (71:316)

You know the rest: Macey, yes, will have ignored the "prophecies" that Gabriel screamed from the top of the main mast, accompanying them with "frantic gestures" of his arm addressed to the "sacrilegious assailants of his divinity," namely, the white whale. The tragic drowning of the chief mate, Gabriel managed to convince the crew, was the realization of his extra-lucid prediction. Or rather, as Ishmael lucidly explains, it is not Gabriel himself who manages to credit his own divination but rather, and beyond the very credulousness of the crew, the simple structure of intent, the target aim, peculiar to all prophecy: "This terrible event clothed the archangel with added influence; because his credulous disciples believed that he had specifically fore-announced it, instead of only making a general prophecy, which any one might have done, and so have chanced to hit one of many marks in the wide margin allowed" (71:317).

Prophecy is, therefore, not so much a matter of the prophet's credibility as of margins and marks (and it is of marks that the text speaks, not of "aims" or "targets," as the French translation has it, thus choosing not to mark, precisely, and remark a certain lexicon of the trace and of writing here at work).[25]

But back to the letter. *Let me have it*, says Mayhew to Ahab, give me this letter covered with marks—folds and mould as well as writing. Let me have this letter, which the sender has entrusted to a destination that is also bordered with a wide margin and that only death (the death of the addressee or death as postman) seems to be able to reach. In spite of the meanders of its wandering through the ocean, in spite of the belatedness structurally inscribed in its posting (for every mail is potentially addressed to someone who may already be dead), the letter is, in a certain manner, in the process of arriving, if with a certain margin of error: it is, in fact, the captain and not the chief mate who is about to receive it.

But *on the verge of arriving too late, the letter immediately departs again* in a kind of rebound, a counterstroke due to the prophetic Gabriel:

> "Nay, keep it thyself," cried Gabriel to Ahab; "thou art soon going that way."
>
> "Curses throttle thee!" yelled Ahab. "Captain Mayhew, stand by now to receive it"; and taking the fatal missive from Starbuck's hands, he caught it in the slit of the pole, and reached it over towards the boat. But as he did so, the oarsmen expectantly desisted from rowing; the boat drifted a little towards the ship's stern; so that, as if by magic, the letter suddenly ranged along with Gabriel's eager hand. He clutched it in an instant, seized the boat-knife, and impaling the letter on it, sent it thus loaded back into the ship. It feel at Ahab's feet. Then Gabriel shrieked out to his comrades to give way with their oars, and in that manner the mutinous boat rapidly shot away from the Pequod. (71:318)

Return to sender, then. And in this return is marked the prophecy of Ahab's future; he, like Macey, the chief mate of the *Jeroboam*, will perish from having wanted to stop the course of Moby Dick. So Gabriel's prophecy promises to be, at least, sent by return mail. If it ever arrives.

Indeed, how could one be sure that a letter or a posting will ever arrive? That they will not end up, in one way or another, at the "dead-letter office," where, in Melville's eponymous story, Bartleby is found?[26] Similarly, how can one ever be assured that a prophecy will be realized? And inversely, how could one renounce the desire for such assurance?

This singular conversation I had the other day with L. is now coming back to my memory. Do you remember it? We were sitting at a table around a glass of *palínka* (Hungarian brandy), in the midst of innumerable things and pieces of furniture that we had to move, and he was asking whether I had received what he had sent me months earlier. Yes, I said to him, embarrassed, and I apologized for not having answered. I thanked him. But he apologized in turn (and it surprised me at first, it amused me). He said: "Forgive me for not having written to you to warn you that I was sending it to you." Excuse me, he was saying to me, in short, for not writing to you that I was going to write to you . . . Once my surprise had passed, I thought: what mad and magnificent, what infinite postal regression! It deploys, in a way, the impossible fantasy of an ascent further and further back, toward a vanishing anchoring point, in order to ensure the arrival of a posting that remains, however, always to come. In order to ensure its happy arrival, according to L., infinitely to defer the future missive by way of a retrogression without end toward the announcement of its announcement (of its announcement . . .), in order to be sure that it arrives at its destination and at the right time—in order to be sure that I am ready for it, expect it, find it, and read it—it would be, paradoxically, necessary to postpone infinitely its postal collection. One would always have to *send it back, to post it and post it again* [la renvoyer] at once, again and again, in a sort of future anterior always more deeply hollowed.

Thus, any posting [*envoi*] doubly becomes, and from the start, a posting again, a posting back, and a postponement [*renvoi*]. It is ceaselessly postponed for later [*renvoyé à plus tard*], multiplying itself before and ahead of itself, in the manner of a *postal prosthesis*. If this is so, it is because it is infinitely returned to sender. It is because it is sent back and thrown back to the infinite, toward its *posting point*, which it hollows out of the stammering abyss of a retroprospection.

Such is the law, the mad law that seems to govern postal desire and the promise of prophecy. Such is the law, the mad law, of their propagation and their *conduction*: like the electricity of the meteoric lightning, the instant—or rather the instance—of *arriving* is spread in waves, forward and backward and inversely. This is why the extraordinary postal scene of *Moby-Dick* can provide us with a reading of the temporal entanglement at work in any sending in general, as well as in what I would call the prophetic *emission* (to be distinguished from the prophetic mission).

# Through the Tomb

EVERYTHING I AM TELLING YOU by intercepting and interrupting those found narratives, my entire tale, made of fragments and glosses of other tales—all this had begun I no longer know when. But I do remember it began with a question—*What day is it today?*— followed, in the guise of a response, by a word whose internal repetition in two languages (one "dead," as they say, the other "living") I like: *aujourd'hui*, a French adverb that, my dictionary explains, includes as its last syllable the Latin *hodie*, "in this day" (from *hoc* and *die*).

Today, it is a day singular among all days, one that repeats itself today. It is today—on the day of this day (*hodie*)—that everything began; that for the first time I have not ceased speaking to you, in spite (or because) of all the interruptions that have separated us. Today is an anniversary.

On the day before, I would never have believed that tomorrow, that all the tomorrows since, that the tomorrows still to come, would be the eve, the approach, and the waking of everything that for me does not cease to echo and resound again since this other today that both recedes into the past and always, every day, shines as it departs for the unknown.

Like the glow-worm of a marvelous short story by Melville, "The Apple-Tree Table," I have just read today, on this very day. I want immediately to address its reading to you, even if I may have to continue tomorrow.

The story—and what a story!—begins with these words: "When I first . . ." (ATT, 378). Very quickly, the narrator comes to tell of his "fascination" (ATT, 383), whose effects are felt first in his hair, as if they were the site of a strange phenomenon of electric conduction or propagation: "My hair began to have a sensation." The disheveled story, which I am about to divert for you, has therefore begun with hairs. On a day that was—that is or will be—today.

What is it, then, that fascinates the narrator? It is first of all the reading of a book, found on an apple-tree table in his old attic: "a ghostly dismantled old quarto" (ATT, 378), a "mouldy old book"— Cotton Mather's *Magnalia Christi Americana*, about which I will tell you more later on (ATT, 380). Once brought down to the living room, both book and table attract the narrator as if by magnetism. His eyes are strained from so much reading. He knows he will have to pay on the next day for the abuse he inflicts upon them, but he continues to read, to read again, and to "read on and on" (ATT, 383).

All of a sudden, as if provoked by this uninterrupted reading, a noise, a kind of "ticking," is heard. Numb with fear, the narrator considers the various potential sources of this noise, which he dismisses one by one. The pendulum of his "great Strasbourg clock" is immobile. His own watch is stored somewhere else. Could it be, from the paneling, a "death tick"—I do not know how to translate this into French (even less given the context, which adds no more precise details), perhaps a kind of fatal countdown, a "ticking of death"? No, he concludes, after having gone "all round the room, holding my ear to the wainscot" (ibid.).

The solution to this spectral riddle, which terrorizes the narrator, will only be found at the end. I renounce trying to render for you the anxious awaiting that animates him throughout these pages—he spends entire nights listening for the return of the noise, in "a condition of intense auricular suspense" (ATT, 388)—and I give you at once the key to the mystery: it is a kind of glow-worm, a "sparkling object" (ATT, 389) in the process of burrowing its way through the wood of the table to find a passage to the light of day. (Or rather, since its countdown seems to manifest itself at late hours: to the darkness of night, which, once out, it will contribute to illuminate).

To those who, incredulous, counter that the table is "at least a hundred years old" and that no living creature could ever come through such old and hardened matter, the narrator replies: "Have not live toads been found in the hearts of dead rocks, as old as creation?" (ATT, 393). Refraining from going so far, "the eminent naturalist" consulted in the last pages will establish through his computations that "the glorious, lustrous, flashing live opal" will have come through "one hundred and fifty years' entombment" (ATT, 397).

If my own computations are correct, this sends us back more or less to the time of the book that seems to have provoked this uncanny affair, namely, Cotton Mather's *Magnalia*, first published in 1702, in the early period of the colonial history of the United States. In this volume, what is at issue are ghosts and specters.

# Spectral Evidence

BUT WHO IS THIS Cotton Mather, and who are these spirits of his? Born in 1663 (his father, Increase Mather, was a renowned pastor in Boston), dead in 1728, he was one of the major clerical figures of early New England Puritan society. Aspiring to succeed to his ancestors, the Reverend Richard Mather and John Cotton, themselves renowned ministers of the sect during the founding generation of the Massachusetts Bay colony, he encountered an obstacle that stood temporarily in the way of his vocation: Mather had to overcome the stammering from which he suffered. Cotton Mather, one might say, resembled a sort of stammering Father Mapple.

He was the author of hundreds of volumes (some dedicated to scientific or medical matters, such as smallpox and its prevention by inoculation) and was admired as well as controversial (Benjamin Franklin—him again—visited Mather and was inspired by his so-called ethical writings). To this day, he also remains associated, if in an ambiguous manner, with the Salem witch trials. For this "doleful, ghostly, ghastly Cotton Mather," as the narrator of "The Apple-Tree Table" has it, was a staunch believer in witches, and he played an active and contested role in their hunting (ATT, 383). "In the most straightforward way, he laid before me detailed accounts of New England witchcraft," many cases of which "he himself had been eyewitness." In short, "Cotton Mather testified whereof he had seen." So says the narrator before asking himself: "But, is it possible?" (ATT, 382).

Is it possible, indeed, to be an ocular witness of the work of spirits, whether they be good or evil? And what would "having seen" mean here?

This question interests me primarily because, mutatis mutandis, it has to do with what would constitute evidence toward supporting a prophecy (of prophecy) in reading. This is a thorny question, no doubt, and Mather knew that better than anyone, having made public pronouncements on numerous occasions and in all kinds of contradictory manners regarding the use of proof and evidence during witchcraft trials.

The first accusations and denunciations of witches in Salem began during the winter of 1691–92. Two jurists led the investigation of these first cases: the first was a certain John Hathorne, the great-grandfather of the writer, Melville's friend Nathaniel Hawthorne.[27] The trials of the accused (male and female), increasingly numerous, began on June 2, 1692, in front of a court gathered for the occasion by the governor, William Phips. On June 10, the first woman was hanged. On June 19, five more. August 19, four men and one woman. September 19, one man—Giles Corey—who had refused to answer the questions of the court and died crushed under the massive quantity of stones that were piled upon him so that he would yield. On September 22, six women and two men were also hanged. After that, the witch hunt decreased like an ebbing tide. There were no more executions. But what the tide left uncovered was more than a doubt. It was a growing culpability.

In fact, the suspicion that innocents had been sent to their deaths had emerged very early, immediately after the first hanging, when Governor Phips had turned to the ministers of the church to ask them for advice. On June 15, they answered him with a declaration that was in all likelihood composed by Cotton Mather, warning the governor against the use of "spectral evidence."

What is this about? What is this "spectral evidence" (as it is called by American historians and jurists)? What is this unbelievable thing that calls, therefore, for infinite belief?

I read the eight-point declaration of the ministers, sent, as it were, by return mail to the governor. It is entitled "The Return," that is to say, no doubt, the reply of "Several Ministers Consulted by his Excellency, and the Honorable Council, upon the Present Witch-crafts in Salem Village." In this return, which was also the beginning of a reversal in the witch-hunt, all the signatories first assert their support of the general cause of the trials.

> II. We cannot but with all Thankfulness acknowledge, the Success which the Merciful God has given unto the Sedulous and Assidu-ous Endeavors of our Honorable Rulers, to detect the Abominable Witchcrafts which have been Committed in the Country; Humbly praying that the Discovery of those Mysterious and Mischievous Wickednesses, may be perfected."[28]

But already in the next point, the ministers give voice to their suspi-cions regarding the well-founded justifications for these condemna-tions. They call for exceeding vigilance in the use of convicting evidence.

> III. We judge that in the prosecution of these, and such Witch-crafts, there is need of a very critical and Exquisite Caution, lest by too much Credulity for Things, received only upon the Devils authority, there be a Door opened for a long Train of miserable Consequences. . . .
> VI. Presumptions whereupon Persons may be Committed, and much more, Convictions upon persons may be Condemned as Guilty of Witchcrafts, ought certainly to be more considerable than barely the Accused Persons being Represented by a Spectre unto the Afflicted; inasmuch as 'tis an undoubted and a Notorious Thing, That a Demon may, by Gods Permission, appear even to Ill purposes, in the Shape of an Innocent, yea, and a virtuous man. Nor can we esteem Alterations made in the Sufferers, by a Look or Touch of the Accused to be an Infallible Evidence of Guilt.

The evidence said to be spectral is therefore the testimony of a person who is described as "afflicted," that is, tormented by the appa-rition of the accused witch in the form of a specter. Those upon whom the suspicion of witchcraft weighs are thus somehow "represented" at the court by a double delegation of their person. They appear or co-appear [*il ou elle comparaît*] in court not only "in person," in order to be interrogated and to respond for their actions (if it is the case that there is a matter of acting here), but also "in the person" (if it is one) of a spirit, a ghost who transforms the body and soul of a third.

The question of spectral evidences establishing the crime of witchcraft is also broached by Cotton Mather's father, Increase Mather, in a volume considered to have contributed to containing the spread of the witch hunt in Salem.[29] Starting on October 3, 1692, Mather the father circulated the manuscript of this book, which he published the following month, entitled *Cases of Conscience Concerning Evil Spirits Personating Men*. At stake is therefore a matter of spirits that pretend to be, that fraudulently simulate, that play and impersonate (or *personate*) the semblance of man. In his archaic English, Mather opposes, with many biblical citations and exegeses, "that which refers to something vulgarly called *Spectre Evidence*."

I do not doubt for an instant the accuracy and the justice [*de la justesse et de la justice*] of this cause, of this warning, which assuredly contributed to hold back the wave of abusive condemnations. Besides, the last sentences of Increase Mather's book are without ambiguity in the matter. The "Jurors," he said, quoting yet another book written by one of his "Acquaintances," must not "Condemn any party Suspected upon bare Presumptions," for they would run the risk of being themselves "guilty through their own Rashness of Shedding Innocent Blood."[30] Still, I must admit that what continues to fascinate me is the very idea of a *spectrality* of the criminal evidence. In cases of witchcraft (as, by the way, in cases of prophecy, which Mather considers proximate to witchcraft as a form of possession by the devil),[31] in fact, everything occurs as if the crime was stripped of its factual elements—since they are all suspected of being diabolical illusions—[32] and reduced to a pure *intentionality*: to a pure *spirit*, therefore. The only evidence considered absolutely valid is henceforth the confession, freely agreed to. It is a *retrospective* declaration of intent.[33]

But then—and this is what Mather the father obviously fails to consider in his argument—from this guilty retrospection that confession is, how is one to establish with certainty that those who present themselves as repentant are the very same human persons who, in person, would have knowingly intended to afflict a third? Otherwise put, how is one to ensure that a *retroprofession of diabolical faith* is not itself haunted or spectral?

The juridical or political *person*, Hannah Arendt recalls in *On Revolution* (where she dedicates a few important pages to Melville's "Billy Budd"), is a mask.[34] She writes:

> In its original meaning, [the Latin word *persona*] signified the mask ancient actors used to wear in a play. . . . The mask as such obviously had two functions: it had to hide, or rather to replace, the actor's own face and countenance, but in a way that would make it possible for the voice to sound through. At any rate, it was in this twofold understanding of a mask through which a voice sounds that the word *persona* became a metaphor and was carried from the language of the theatre into legal terminology. The distinction between a private individual in Rome and a Roman citizen was that the latter had a *persona*, a legal personality, as we would say; it was as though the law had affixed to him the part he was expected to play on the public scene, with the provision, however, that his own voice would be able to sound through.[35]

How can one be sure, then, that it is the same voice that, through the mask of the *person*, confesses today the intention it had promised to keep and realize yesterday or the day before? How can one know who speaks, and with what voice, behind a mask? How is one to identify the voices that pass, that transit or, literally, *per-sonate*? In short, how is one to assign or attribute all the voices of a mask when these, in their cohort, form a *hauntology*, doubling, preceding, and counterstriking one another, between today, yesterday, and tomorrow?[36]

# Backfire

I IMAGINE A VOICE in a text that, like the light of a glow-worm digging its way through the ages and marking the countdown (the *death-tick*) of the instant in which it will emerge, would retroprospectively confess that it is returning—it was sent or emitted so long ago—that it is *returning from the future*.

This voice could be Gabriel's, the false prophet who returns to sender the dead letter summoned from the past by one who has trespassed, but reverses it into a prediction that would reach Ahab from the future and about his future.

This voice, though, I hear it more as resembling that of Ahab, the prosthetic and prophetic captain himself. Do you remember the strange and uncanny chapter of *Moby-Dick* entitled "The Candles"? In the middle of a raging storm, in the radiance of Saint Elmo's fire, Ahab—about whom I nonetheless ask myself whether he is in fact himself, if it is Ahab in person rather than a *persona* coming through—invokes directly the igneous spirit, the mortal and meteoric power of lightning. He confesses here and professes his faith, contracting with the diabolical power of fire. He does so by speaking in one stroke, or rather in one breath in return, a kind of *backfire*.

I now know thee, thou clear spirit, and I now know that thy right worship is defiance. To neither love nor reverence wilt thou be kind; and e'en for hate thou canst but kill; and all are killed. No fearless fool now fronts thee. I own thy speechless, placeless power; but to the last gasp of my earthquake life will dispute its unconditional, unintegral mastery in me.[37] In the midst of the personified

75

impersonal, a personality stands there. . . . Oh, thou clear spirit, of thy fire thou madest me, and like a true child of fire, I breathe it back to thee. (119:507)

Ahab is thus standing erect in front of an igneous hearth, which he invokes. And like the host of "The Lightning-Rod Man" in front of his hearthstone (and apart from the apparent quiet), he stands in the to and fro of a burning presence that seems to arrive and touch down only to surge and counterstrike again. Ahab's person defies the fire in person—his "personality," as he puts it himself—and stands *here*: that is to say, it stands in the meteoric back and forth where, straight as an I, "I" becomes a fragile, ascending line that is traversed, in both senses, by the propagation of the fire.

Yet unlike the male and female witches evoked by Mather father and son, unlike the traditional figure of the possessed or of the prophet (whom he otherwise resembles so closely), Ahab does not address himself to—nor does he receive anything from—the beyond. The fire he invokes is no transcendence. Listen to Ahab apostrophizing it:

Yet blindfold, yet will I talk to thee. Light though thou be, thou leapest out of darkness; but I am darkness leaping out of light, leaping out of thee! . . . But thou art but my fiery father; my sweet mother I know not. Oh, cruel! What hast thou done with her? There lies my puzzle; but thine is greater. Thou knowest not how came ye, hence callest thyself unbegotten; certainly knowest not thy beginning, hence callest thyself unbegun. I know that of me, which thou knowest not of thyself, oh, thou omnipotent. There is some unsuffusing thing beyond thee, thou clear spirit, to whom all thy eternity is but time, all thy creativeness mechanical.[38] Through thee, thy flaming self, my scorched eyes do dimly see it. (119:507–8)

Ahab returns fire with fire, blowing back fire to fire. Yet it is also beyond fire that Ahab sends fire back: into fire, issued and coming from fire, apprehended and comprehended by fire, he becomes, in a way, greater than fire. He overtakes it, he *comprehends* it in his turn, and he sees through it, even if darkly. The creature that fire has created, the creature that has surged from fire, sees through it to the dark origin from which fire itself came, of which it is ignorant. Darkness, greater than the light of fire it originally contains, darkness finds itself again in this *enclosure*, in this prosthetic and prophetic being to whom fire has, in turn, given birth: Ahab.

But this beyond fire—in relation to which fire's "eternity is but time"—is no transcendence. Which is to say that it does not bring one out of the world into the beyond of another world: *behind the fire, there is no hors-texte.* Otherwise put, by dimly seeing the darkness whence comes the fire from which he has himself issued, Ahab does not pierce with his gaze, he does not see through this "wall," which he had earlier described as his prison. As Ahab was beginning to suspect, "there's naught beyond" this wall, which—I was suggesting this to you—is nothing but the outline or the limit of the text as whale.

You see—if it remains at all possible to see anything in this vicinity where our eyes are burning—the spirit of the fire may be, for Ahab, this flame that lights the way toward the hunt of the white whale. Which is to say, literally, toward *Moby-Dick*, toward the book itself, here under my eyes, which I am reading to you. The spirit of fire, for this textual being that Ahab is, is perhaps this paradoxical light projected toward a *hors-texte* that would be nothing other than the unattainable totality of the text itself. It is a blinding white light, and therefore an obscure light, like that of Leviathan, like that of lightning, too.

The Leviathan-text could be dimly seen in this way, in short bursts, by the light of the lightning bolt that, illuminating what remains to come of the text, is sent back and sent again in its very posting toward the future anterior of retroprophecies. And this posting, this double posting, through which the luminous tear of the text is both repeated and deferred (it is posted and sent again, postponed), is inscribed here and there in the figures of postal returns to sender, of returning strokes and backfires. Always I feel that, crouching behind these signs or symptoms, the prophetic speech of the Leviathan-text anticipates—and therefore delays—itself, ahead of itself as its own exteriority.

Everything, in the Leviathan-text, can therefore become a prophetic mark. And every text, insofar as it is one, is no doubt endowed with something of a leviathanic attribute—the privilege of *Moby-Dick* being that it renders this dimension exemplarily thematic. Or better: this *hyper-dimension [surdimension]* of the text vis-à-vis itself—its overflowing.

Hence, between the text and its future, *the prophecy of the text* (hear this in the irreducible ambiguity of an oscillating genitive, between the objective and the subjective, between a text that would be object or subject of its own prediction or prescription) predicts nothing that awaits its realization. This is the event of reading, which, when it comes, when it rushes like lightning, electrifies retroprospectively the chains and the lines, interrupting them, rearranging them in an unprecedented fashion by the force of its magnetism. This is why the instant prophecy *takes* has the structure of a back and forth at the speed of lightning: the event that comes from the future—from these readings for you that I defer in order to watch over them as in a waking dream—reads retroprospectively the past, one that will henceforth shine with a thousand sparkles [*éclat*], each of which seems to call in advance, to call forth the lightning [*éclair*] to come.

In short, a voice comes out of its muteness and speaks through the text: through this immense prosthetic and prophetic mask that, like a strange and monstrous *persona*, masks nothing but itself.

# Isolation, the Bubble, and the Future of the Text

I REMEMBER ONE DAY WHEN (will you forgive me?) I overheard one of your conversations on the telephone: you were speaking of yourself—of each of us—as of an island, and to the other voice, which was no doubt protesting, you replied laughing, as if by an ironic concession, that we were all, minimally and in any case, peninsulas.

This is also the way in which Father Mapple's audience is described in *Moby-Dick*. Each of them is like an islet. Each of them could be part of an archipelago. The audience awaiting Father Mapple in the chapel is, in fact, presented as a congregation of atoms properly *isolated*: "Each silent worshipper seemed purposely sitting apart from the other, as if each silent grief were insular and incommunicable. The chaplain had not yet arrived; and there these silent islands of men and women sat steadfastly" (7:34).

When Father Mapple enters among these juxtaposed, awaiting insularities, in the midst of an archipelago composed of "I's" as numerous as the pairs of ears, he begins by isolating himself in the pulpit, in a manner that is, to say the least, remarkable.

Like most old fashioned pulpits, it was a very lofty one, and since a regular stairs to such a height would, by its long angle with the floor, seriously contract the already small area of the chapel, the architect, it seemed, had acted upon the hint of Father Mapple, and finished the pulpit without a stairs, substituting a perpendicular side ladder. . . . Halting for an instant at the foot of the ladder,

. . . Father Mapple cast a look upwards, and then with a truly
sailor-like but still reverential dexterity, hand over hand, mounted
the steps as if ascending the main-top of his vessel. . . .

I was not prepared to see Father Mapple after gaining the
height, slowly turn round, and stooping over the pulpit, deliber-
ately drag up the latter step by step, till the whole was deposited
within, leaving him impregnable in his little Quebec. . . .

Can it be, then, that by that act of physical isolation, he signifies
his spiritual withdrawal for the time, from all outward worldly ties
and connexions? Yes, for replenished with the meat and wine of
the word, to the faithful man of God, this pulpit, I see, is a self-
containing stronghold. (8:39)

From this fortress, from this inner forum or fort [*for ou fort inté-
rieur*], there will surge a prophetic sermon that you already know,
namely, a reading of the story of Jonah, a kind of prosthesis or pro-
thesis, an enclosure within *Moby-Dick*, a kind of anticipated fore-
position of the story to come, that of Moby Dick and the tragic hunt
for him. The pulpit is, besides, described as an outpost [*avant-poste*]
toward that which is coming:

Its panelled front was in the likeness of a ship's bluff bows, and
the Holy Bible rested on a projecting piece of scroll work, fashioned after a ship's fiddle-headed beak.

What could be more full of meaning?—for the pulpit is ever
this earth's foremost part; all the rest comes in its rear; the pulpit
leads the world. From thence it is the storm of God's quick wrath
is first descried, and the bow must bear the earliest brunt. From
thence it is the God of breezes fair or foul is first invoked for
favorable winds. Yes, the world's a ship on its passage out, and not
a voyage complete; and the pulpit is its prow. (8:40)

Like the host of "The Lightning-Rod Man," from the hearth of
his pulpit, Father Mapple reads the storm to come, the storm that is
the future. Or at least he perceives its foreboding winds; he receives
its aura, the breeze before the storm. It is in this manner that he can
forecast it, foreread [*prélire*] it in scripture, in the book that is itself

lying on a kind of pier, a *jetée*, a "projecting piece" (which I would have liked to translate as a *projetée*).

Sometimes I dream of being able to read or foreread, after the manner of Father Mapple, of being able to decipher the tongues of submarine earth that, secretly, connect our insularities. I dream of the just prayer that, like the psalm he finally strikes up in front of the archipelago of his auditors, would let me reach into the sea bed, its deep or shallow shoals, which, always submerged, are extended between us: "a prayer so deeply devout that he seemed kneeling and praying at the bottom of the sea" (9:41).

What would there be, *at bottom*, between you and me, that would make of each of us, not peninsulas (I cannot manage to see a continent), but atolls or reefs emerging from a subaquatic architecture? This question no doubt moves my stories of stories [*mes récits de récits*], it makes them navigate from reef to reef [*de récif en récif*], at the risk of breaking into discontinuous shards. Still, I am afraid of thinking that I could be seeing, seeing dimly or foreseeing, like Pip during his dive, the "wondrous depth, where strange shapes of the unwarped primal world" would be gliding (93:414): in short, the abyss I imagine lying between our insularities.

Would we be mobile islets, then, monadic enclosures adrift in the midst of a vast ocean, on or under the undulating surface from which run Leviathan-texts that swell until they seem to comprehend everything?

I feel that I am dangerously approaching the end. From the moment Ishmael finds himself, like Pip, floating alone on the flood, like a land without anchor pushed by the currents. From the instant when, perhaps, the whale-text would be on the verge of exploding, swollen with its accumulated substance, like static electricity.

In *Moby-Dick*, the writing of the end is presented both as the end of writing and as its beginning anew. Or its beginning, period.

I have to tell you in detail about the last chapters, not only in order to hold you back still, in extremis, but also because all the successive prophecies of all the prophetic figures of the novel are here coming undone, accomplishing themselves as in a chain. You know all these figures, I have introduced them all to you—all except one, and it is perhaps the most striking.

I am talking about Fedallah. This uncanny character appears suddenly when Ahab decides for the first time to lower his boat. Until then, Fedallah had remained hidden, along with four other sailors, forming what Ishmael describes as a phantom crew, "subordinate phantoms" (50:230). Fedallah is the most mysterious among these five, who constitute a sort of close guard for Ahab. In Ishmael's eyes, there is in him something of "the ghostly aboriginalness of earth's primal generations" (50:231). In him, there appears to surge something of the ghost of the origin as a ghostly origin, of the mythic time that immediately followed Genesis, "when the memory of the first man was a distinct recollection, and all men his descendants, unknowing whence he came, eyed each other as real phantoms" (ibid.)

Other members of the Pequod's regular crew see in Fedallah an incarnation of the devil. But Fedallah, in truth, is above all the voice of Ahab's fate, which he announces in a cryptic manner. One night, Ahab suddenly wakes up, startled, to find himself face to face with Fedallah. Both are "hooped round by the gloom of the night," as if they were "the last men in a flooded world" (117:498). Ahab asks Fedallah about his dream and the latter's replies, like those of an oracle, are so many encrypted prophecies of the end. His sentences, in fact, literally contain the program according to which *Moby-Dick* will end.

> "I have dreamed it again," said [Ahab].
>
> "Of the hearses? Have I not said, old man, that neither hearse nor coffin can be thine?" . . .
>
> "But I said, old man, that ere thou couldst die on this voyage, two hearses must verily be seen by thee on the sea; the first not made by mortal hands; and the visible wood of the last one must be grown in America" (117:498–99)

This prediction for Ahab is also accompanied by a kind of self-prophecy by which Fedallah declares that he will always be "before" his captain ("I shall still go before thee"), that he will be, as it were, his "pilot" even unto death, in which he will precede him.

In fact, in the last chapters of *Moby-Dick*, one witnesses the point by point realization of Fedallah's enigmatic prediction. Thus, on the second day of the final chase, after the white whale has overturned both boats and men, Fedallah disappears. He reappears in the following chapter, as the men scream in horror. What they see then is, in fact, Fedallah's corpse, half torn, "lashed round and round to the fish's back, pinioned in the turns upon turns in which, during the past night, the whale had reeled the involutions of the lines around him" (135:568).

The dénouement of *Moby-Dick* is approaching, and the hour has come for the verification of all accumulated prophecies. Ahab says this clearly when he addresses Fedallah's ghost, attached to the whale: "Aye, and thou goest before; and this, *this* then is the hearse that thou didst promise" (ibid.). But this last hour in which the various lines—fishing lines and reading lines, anchor lines and lines of flight or lines of divination—are more intertwined that ever, forming turns and knots ("involutions"), this ultimate hour is also, and at the same time, that in which the lines are broken and torn: when the white whale, harpooned again, "darted through the weltering sea," then "the treacherous line . . . snapped in the empty air" (135:569–70).

The end is near, predicted and yet unpredictable. The lines are tied, taut, and they break. The unexpected occurs, as the radically improbable verification of the prophecy: the white whale charges upon the *Pequod* itself, which, shipwrecked and engulfing the entire crew, becomes the hearse made of American wood prophesied by Fedallah.

Then, surrounding the wreckage, "the great shroud of the sea rolled on as it rolled five thousand years ago" (135:572).

In "The Lightning-Rod Man" as well, at the end, "the scroll of the storm is rolled back" (LRM, 124) and writing is gathered, closing upon itself while promising its repetition. In *Moby-Dick*, after the tying and the breaking of lines, this rolling and unrolling motion of the sea ("the sea rolled on") covers the scene and completes the tale while announcing a loop back to its beginning. The shroud covers the text that has been written until now, as if it had become a corpse. But this pale veil is also a kind of page, white and virginal, upon which all can be reinscribed.

"The drama's done," says the first sentence of the brief epilogue that follows, but there is one survivor of the wreck: Ishmael, who has found refuge in the "coffin life-buoy," will drift for a few days, between life and death, before being rescued by another ship.

The exergue for this epilogue is a citation from the Bible, from the book of Job: "And I only am escaped alone to tell thee" (Job 1:15–19).

Here, at the end, when everything is already written and narrated, writing will therefore begin—begin again. Ishmael the survivor can henceforth write the novel *Moby-Dick*, once the novel is completed. Ishmael has seen the end of the world. He has seen the ship sink, of which nothing was saved. No ark, no rainbow, no protection or lightning rod: Ishmael has, in a way, come through death itself, through the death so often announced and prophesied. Unlike Noah, not only has he been unable to save anything, but he also finds nothing new after the wreck. He has survived in a coffin, from which he emerges in order to write that which one already knows, that which I have already told you and read.

Listen again to how Ishmael tells his survival *in extremis*. The "suction" of the wrecked ship, he says, draws him "towards the closing vortex." Turning round and round, Ishmael comes closer to the "black bubble at the axis of that slowly wheeling circle." But as he is about to reach it, the bubble bursts and throws out the coffin, that is, the funeral buoy, which will enable him to survive as living-dead, to write that which is already written.

In the maelstrom of this generalized shipwreck, everything occurs as if, with Ishmael's coffin, the Leviathan-text is contriving within itself a kind of ultimate bubble. At the moment it seems to touch upon its limit or its end, it proves to enclose within itself the promise or the prophecy of itself, as a text yet to be written.

Such is no doubt, *in fine*, the last figure of the double enclosure in which I have sought to grasp the emergence of prophecy. The text includes its promise of writing, which itself contains it as a prophecy to come.

Writing is only prophetic in the renewed beginning in which it truly begins. Reading too will be so in rereading.

There is nothing to verify, nothing to predict. Everything has already been, everything has already occurred. And everything can be rewritten and reread, precisely because everything has already taken place.

Everything, therefore, remains to be said. Everything to tell.

I listen to you now. It is your turn.

# Post-Scriptum: On Whiteness and Beheading

WAIT.

Just a few more words, in front of the poster—or rather, its memory—through which everything has happened.

A few words before it is, perhaps, in the generalized shipwreck, completely washed away by the sea, much like Noah's placards, which lie at the bottom of the Pequod's hold.

Do you remember the announcement?

> *"Grand Contested Election for the Presidency of the United States.*
> "WHALING VOYAGE BY ONE ISHMAEL.
> "BLOODY BATTLE IN AFFGHANISTAN."

That whaling voyage is now over. And its story will be able to begin, which is to say, begin again.

The voyage, then, once again.

And on a blank page.

But what is the whiteness of a page?

What is the virginity of paper?

Visiting a "paper-mill," the narrator of another fascinating Melville short story, entitled "The Tartarus of Maids," dreams of the uses to come for the sheets freshly produced by the machines: "Looking at that blank paper continually dropping, dropping, dropping, my

86

mind ran on in wonderings of those strange uses to which those thousand sheets eventually would be put. All sorts of writings would be writ on those now vacant things—sermons, lawyers' briefs, physicians' prescriptions, love-letters, marriage certificates, bills of divorce, registers of births, death-warrants, and so on, without end" (TM, 333).

Yet in order to produce these sheets destined to receive innumerable signs, it is to the infinite, like the rolling of the sea that washes away all traces, that the mill turns, rolls, unrolls, and pours out its virgin paper pulp, still warm when it is deposited at the end of its passage through the machines. And in the incessant return of this cycle, it is precisely the erasure of one word—of one name—that measures time, that enables the identification of something like a duration in a process eternally repeated. To the narrator "amazed at the elongation, interminable convolutions, and deliberate slowness of the machine" (TM, 332), the guide of the visit proposes to take "a bit of paper," to "mark it with any word you please," and to follow its trajectory from beginning to end. The narrator agrees, and begins to move together with the piece of paper, whose motion he watches over "inch by inch." He awaits as it disappears and reappears under cylinders that are often impenetrable ("as it disappeared beneath inscrutable groups of the lower cylinders"), until it finally emerges, "an unfolded sheet of perfect foolscap," with the word (the name) "half faded out of it" (ibid.).

The paper's trajectory is a journey, like Ishmael's ("my travels were at an end," he says, "for here was the end of the machine" ). And when, answering his guide's question, this visitor-traveler declares: "nine minutes to a second," he is seized with "a curious emotion," one "not wholly unlike that which one might experience at the fulfillment of some mysterious prophecy." In its prosthetic precision, the accomplishment of a prophecy has something mechanical about it. And as in *Moby-Dick*, the space of reading a trail or a traced destiny is here bounded and marked, measured by way of an inscription and its erasure: an instant from which, retroprospectively, the future begins, as it were, to *pace and measure* [arpenter] the past.

One can hear a certain irony, no doubt, when the narrator evokes "that celebrated comparison of John Locke," who, "in demonstration of his theory that man had no innate ideas," described "the human mind at birth" as "a sheet of blank paper" (TM, 333). Whiteness and virginity are everywhere marked and remarked in this gripping little tale—it is in fact by traveling through a landscape of snow and ice that the visitor reaches the factory, whose whitewashed walls shelter pale young women working and reproducing, white upon white, the general paleness.[39] And yet there is nonetheless, at the heart of this story's white writing, a paragraph that, even more than the episode of the half-effaced word, erases, as it were, whiteness itself. Discreetly but definitively, this paragraph wears down or ruins the purity or alleged virginity.

Here it is.

The narrator, who has just followed, step by step, all the meanderings of the white paper's genesis—the immense vats filled with white pulp, the rolls, the innumerable cylinders—is now afraid of this gigantic automaton:

> Something of awe now stole over me, as I gazed upon this inflexible iron animal. Always, more or less, machinery of this ponderous, elaborate sort strikes, in some moods, strange dread into the human heart, as some living, panting Behemoth might. But what made the thing I saw so specially terrible to me was the metallic necessity, the unbudging fatality which governed it. Though, here and there, I could not follow the thin, gauzy vail of pulp in the course of its more mysterious or entirely invisible advance, yet it was indubitable that, at those points where it eluded me, it still marched on in unvarying docility to the autocratic cunning of the machine. A fascination fastened on me. I stood spell-bound and wandering in my soul. Before my eyes—there, passing in slow procession along the wheeling cylinders, I seemed to see, glued to the pallid incipience of the pulp, the yet more pallid faces of all the pallid girls I had eyed that heavy day. Slowly, mournfully, beseechingly, yet unresistingly, they gleamed along, their agony dimly outlined on the imperfect paper, like the print of the tormented face on the handkerchief of Saint Veronica. (TM, 333–34)

So, in this story where everything is pale and white, from the paper to the landscape and the faces, paleness and whiteness are not equivalent to a virginity without traces. On the contrary, the apparently virgin sheets are prey to shadows. They are peopled with tracks and imprints, vague and ghostly outlines.

I find myself dreaming, fascinated, with my mind wandering, like the narrator of "The Tartarus of Maids." I am thinking: What were, on our poster, these truly "important" events, those appearing, as if in watermarks, only to serve their function of jewel box, no more than background to Ishmael's "solo"? What were the contested election, the bloody Afghan war, if not pale shadows spectrally appearing on the paper pulp of this placard posted on the prow of our tale?

A kind of pre-scription, no doubt, a *prae-scriptum* that, *in fine*, remains and haunts the reading of the Leviathan-text.

It is here, it is within this beginning, which is also the end, that a political reading of *Moby-Dick* would begin again, a reading attentive to all the ghostly faces, all the livid, living-dead or *praescripta* that inhabit the immense and white surface of the whale-novel.[40]

I am neither the first nor the last to believe himself capable of detecting, under the Leviathan-text, the shadow or the ghost of Thomas Hobbes's *Leviathan*, the first grand modern theory of the State, written in 1651. Besides, Melville himself invites one to do so, with this citation of *Leviathan* figuring among the numerous "allusions to whales" collected in the exergue to *Moby-Dick* (these citations being themselves prosthetic or prescriptive, given their position ahead or at the prow) "By art is created that great LEVIATHAN, called a COMMONWEALTH or STATE—(in Latin, CIVITAS) which is but an artificial man."

*Leviathan*—that is to say, this giant man, this oversized artifice, this prosthesis or mechanical automaton created by covenant, which Hobbes calls the State—is thus explicitly invoked even before the story begins.[41] It is also visible as a watermark at the end, in the epilogue, when Ishmael identifies himself with Job, to say that he alone swims away and remains to narrate. In the Bible—another whale-text—it is, of course, in the book of Job that appears Leviathan of the sea, this teratological figure that forms a sort of monstrous couple with Behemoth, his earthly equivalent. Of the one and the other, Hobbes will have respectively made a symbol of the State and that of anarchy or of revolution.[42]

The title page of Hobbes's *Leviathan*, in the first English edition of 1651, included an engraving that represents a gigantic man, constituted of an infinity of small men. This allegory—intended to illustrate the conception of the Leviathan-state as an artificial man "of greater stature and strength than the Naturall," for whose protection and defense it was intended—makes the page into a poster or a placard that Hobbes composed in close collaboration with his engraver.[43] It makes it into a kind of anticipated echo of the white paper peopled with livid faces at the end of "The Tartarus of Maids," in which the narrator has just compared the immense mechanical apparatus of the paper mill to Behemoth.

Behemoth and Leviathan, but also *Moby-Dick* against—close up against—*Leviathan*: Is there not a barely latent conflict here? Is there not a pitiless war of reading raging between Melville and Hobbes?

On Hobbes's letterhead, on the frontispiece of *Leviathan*, there are "homunculi" that fill "the trunk and the members of the royal giant." They are "seen from the back (as coats and hats), in such manner that they appear to contemplate the face of the monarch of which they form, simultaneously, the body."[44] On Melville's white paper, on the other hand, ghosts are appearing—frontally, it seems—without forming any configuration that would gather or subsume them. They float, one might say, drifting.

Hobbes was, after all, the first to think reading as a political matter or, inversely, to think the political as a question of reading. At the end of his introduction to *Leviathan*, he wrote:

> He that is to govern a whole Nation, must read in himself, not this, or that particular man; but Man-kind: which though it be hard to do, harder than to learn any Language, or Science; yet, when I shall have set down my own reading orderly, and perspicuously, the pains left another, will be onely to consider, if he also find not the same in himself. For this kind of Doctrine, admitteth no other Demonstration.[45]

We might hear, in a passage from *Moby-Dick* (in a chapter entitled "Cetology"), a parody of Hobbes's discourse on the sovereign reading

that would be practiced by the sovereign, for whom "reading in himself" amounts to reading the ensemble of homunculi that compose him, that is, ideally, "mankind." The paragraph of which I am thinking speaks, in fact, of reading under two figures with which we are now familiar, namely, postal sorting (as in the scene with Gabriel the false prophet in chapter 71) and navigation (as in so many evocations of the trail or of sea charts that are found throughout Ishmael's narrative, as well as in Cicero). This paragraph also speaks of mad diving into oceanic depths, the bathymetrical experience that poor Pip underwent during his oracular drowning (chapter 93). It is in this context, therefore, in this contexture that Ishmael weaves and interweaves the different motifs dear to him, that he announces his "cetological" project, which is to say, his idea of a great treatise of leviathanology, whose systematicity or organicity would remain, however, always to come. In short, a kind of *Leviathan* in the minor mode, like a piece of wreckage after the ship has sunk, where the only floating remainder would be the lone architectonic desire, drifting without end and without anchor, without ever reaching the coastal waters of a social contract. Here it is:

I promise nothing complete; because any human thing supposed to be complete, must for that very reason infallibly be faulty. . . . My object here is simply to project the draught of a systematization of cetology. . . .

But it is a ponderous task; no ordinary letter-sorter in the Post-office is equal to it. To grope down into the bottom of the sea after them; to have one's hands among the unspeakable foundations, ribs, and very pelvis of the world; this is a fearful thing. What am I that I should essay to hook the nose of this leviathan! The awful tauntings in Job might well appal me. "Will he (the leviathan) make a covenant with thee? Behold the hope of him is vain!" But I have swam through libraries and sailed through oceans. (32:136)

You will have guessed it in passing: Ishmael has cited, in quotation marks, the Bible. In such a fashion, however, that the reading he offers becomes a reading weapon against Hobbes. For Ishmael selects and sorts what he reads. He erases, elides, and makes us read elliptically a montage composed of distant verses from the book of Job: "Will he make a covenant with thee?" (41:4); "Behold, the hope of him is vain" (41:9). By this reading artifice, eliding and contracting two disjoined lines of the Book, Ishmael manages to make the Bible say that there is no contractual bargaining whatsoever with Leviathan.

No assured contract, therefore, no hook, here, to fasten reading to a Leviathan that would have become a "fast fish," that is to say, anchored, as in Hobbes, in the stable figure of the State.[46] No contract, that is to say, no firm bond or election that, as in Hobbes, delegates the voices of men contractually agreeing among themselves on the sovereign they choose to represent them.[47] No election but a cut. Or better yet, an *elision*, which will reveal itself to be a beheading.

In a later chapter, Ishmael will in fact take care of staging the beheading of Leviathan ("he was beheaded," 70:310). Decapitated, the sovereign Leviathan—who served the function of an inflated, meteoric prosthesis to the unattainable totality promised as much by the text as by the social contract—now resembles the chimney of the "I" in "I and My Chimney." There, the narrator describes it as a "grand seignor," as the "one great domineering object" of the house, and he relates its being cut down to size by a previous owner. This was the equivalent, he says, of a "beheading," a "neck-wringing." It was, he continues, "a regicidal act"[48]

So, for Ishmael as for "I" (I, me), it is in this revolutionary gesture that cuts into the crowning of the all that a space opens where reading is *without end*: without heading, without head. Promised or delivered unto prosthetic and prophetic rereadings that remain always to come.

Once again, it is your turn.

# Ipsology (Selves of Peter Szendy)

## GIL ANIDJAR

I alone have escaped to tell you.

—THE BOOK OF JOB

The very concept of a thing in itself—of reality independent of ideality—
is the survival of a prehistoric personification. Hence even the
staunchest positivist is unwittingly an animist.

—CHRISTOPHER BRACKEN

FOR SCIENCE AT LARGE, the Copernican revolution (from Copernicus down to faithful, or less faithful, reiterations of his name) was supposed to have actualized the paradoxical possibility of thinking "what there can effectively be when there is no thought [*ce qu'il peut effectivement y avoir lorsqu'il n'y a pas de pensée*]," that is to say, what not only precedes but exceeds human thought and cognition.[1] By making knowledge conform to the object rather than the object conform to knowledge, the revolution brought about and carried through a decentering of knowledge away from the human subject (118).[2] As Freud famously articulated it (Kant's own claim clearly notwithstanding), this was a revolution that occurred not once but three times, rehearsing Copernicus's gesture with the same consequences every time and bringing thereby an increasingly assured end to anthropocentrism, perhaps even to humanism. Or so it seemed. In each case, at any rate, there emerged the primacy of the other, an object or an order (cosmic, natural, or sociopsychical) that precedes or exceeds the human, temporally and otherwise, and within which the human subject might be included—or not. This object or order was, at any rate, no longer *contingent* on the human, much less on the subject. Instead, man "himself"—the human, knowing subject— found therein his contingency, the condition of his possibility, and, better (or worse), the plausibility of his expendability.

For the truth or falsity of a physical law is not established with regard to our own existence—whether we exist or do not exist has no bearing upon its truth. Certainly, the presence of an observer may eventually affect the effectuation of a physical law, as is the case for some of the laws of quantum physics—but the very fact that an observer can influence the law is itself a property of the law, which is not supposed to depend upon the existence of an observer. (114)

This insight, which Quentin Meillassoux oddly confines to science (here physics, but mathematics as well, dominates his account, even when he invokes fossils as "what may be while we are not"; 115), has to do with the possibility of thinking and/or knowing an "absolute"—again, an object or order that is what it is or becomes while fundamentally *absolved* of its relation to the human and perhaps of all relations (hence, absolute).[3] In a manner reminiscent of Hannah Arendt's description of "this event, second in importance to no other," whereby the knowledge came that "mankind will not remain bound to the earth forever," Meillassoux proposes that we understand the Copernican revolution (or indeed, revolutions) as the precisely reversed possibility, namely, that the earth—indeed, the world as we know and inhabit it—might not remain bound to mankind forever.[4] Insofar as it constitutes "a world that is *separable* from man," earth (or the universe) is "more indifferent than ever to human existence, and hence indifferent to whatever knowledge humanity might have of it." Earth, the entire world of beings and things, possesses, in other words, "a power of persistence and permanence that is completely unaffected by our existence or inexistence" (115–116). As the title of a recent, highly popular book has it, it always promises (or threatens) to be a "world without us."[5] Increasingly so.

Meillassoux does not stop at this, however. He goes on to puzzle over the massive and collective recoil he perceives, the step back and backward that followed, perhaps even shadowing from the very start, the Copernican breakthroughs. Rather than maintaining its nonanthropocentric impetus (as science presumably has), philosophy proceeded to conduct "a Ptolemaic counter-revolution," to uphold a worldview whereby nothing would be available to thought outside of its relationship to the human subject (118). (This is where Meillassoux connects with Michel Foucault, among others, and to the centrality of man, which Foucault identifies as coextensive with modernity, not only with philosophy). Beginning with Kant, now paradoxically to be thought of as an old reactionary, it seems to have become impossible to think anything independently of man, anything like an object or an "order of things" bearing no relation to the human, something that might be called an absolute.[6] What happened instead is "correlationism," a generalized and dominant mode of thought and knowledge incapable "of accounting for the noncorrelational scope of mathematics, which is to say, for the very existence of science, the latter being properly understood as the power to decenter thought" (121).

In other words, for philosophy, as Meillassoux has it, everything has become conditional, embedded and enmeshed in webs and networks of relationality. More specifically, nothing is thinkable any longer outside of a relation (or co-relation) to the knowing subject, and better yet (although Meillassoux does not linger on this active, constitutive dimension), outside of a relation to the *active* and *productive* human subject.[7] As Giambattista Vico put it, and as many confirmed after him, thereby sealing the central inheritance of the Cartesian co-agitating *cogito*, men can only know that which they have made and produced.[8] Knowledge, along with history, became ever more grounded in the human, laboring subject (even if the relation between thought and being cannot be reduced to the relation subject-object; 7). The order of beings and things became correlational, increasingly and almost exclusively understood as construction and invention, agency and self-fashioning, and man was quietly (or not so quietly perhaps) reinstated as lord and maker of the universe, even if thereby to find himself within an inextricable and differential network of relations, from which there was to be no absolution (it is thus, Meillassoux explains, that "transcendental idealism" won the day; 121). The ties that bind never seemed so unbreakable. In any event, nothing henceforth would ever come about outside of human purview and control, and minimally independent of a relation to it. Things and objects, indeed, nature "herself" (who might well abide by immutable laws), all became unavailable to a conception, even an existence, that would be free of human agency, whether psychical or material, individual or collective.

This explains why, even as the nonhuman sciences grew, the indisputable culmination of scientific achievements after Copernicus could take the actualized form of a fantasy—space travel—whereby the earth might disappear, but not mankind. Ever more immortal and ever further from endorsing his soon-to-come and subsequently long-gone erasure, "like a face drawn in sand at the edge of the sea,"[9] man appears not to have ceased reasserting his centrality and unexpendability (his immortality) under the guise of "correlationism" (Emmanuel Levinas called it, I think, "imperialism"). As Meillassoux puts it, we live in a Ptolemaic universe, in which nothing exists outside—or independently—of our knowing, watchful, and all too human eye, free of our interventionist and ever so constructive hand.[10]

Under the heading of a "speculative materialism" (121), what Meillassoux is asking us to consider—beginning with the absolute as that which is absolved of all (human) relations—does not have to be restricted to the natural sciences. I was trying to suggest as much when evoking the figure of the other (not just the ontic realm of fossils, or even the universe or mathematical absolutes, as Meillassoux has it) as preceding and exceeding the subject.[11] Within the correlational tradition that Meillassoux identifies (some will say that he performs and even makes up), it seems that one can most definitely find, within philosophy and elsewhere, a number of attempts at testifying to that which exceeds thought, to that which must be registered in the absence of the human subject—though the nature of this record (and of that absence as well) will have to come, later on, under scrupulous interrogation. There are, at any rate, reasons to await Meillassoux's forthcoming work before pronouncing further judgment,[12] before evaluating what might be his engagement with Foucault's "thought of the outside," for example, or with other attempts to think "these occurrences of matter independent of humanity [ces événements d'une matière sans homme]," occurrences of which science speaks, along with a number of other disciplines and discourses (18). For now, it might suffice to say that it is the anti- or nonhumanism of science that Meillassoux lingers on, the strenuous *indifference* of science (and of its objects) to human existence.[13] It may be, too, that a different concern, at least at the manifest level a different *ethical* concern, animates him and those who have asked the question "Who comes after the subject?"[14] For the decentering of the subject Meillassoux underscores by way of temporality (the fossil that preceded the human will also outlast it) may have less to do with precedence than with that which (already) persists and insists regardless of human existence, indifferent to it. Recall that Meillassoux is preoccupied with "the arche-fossil," as he calls it, namely, with the "manifestation of the world that is posited as anterior to the emergence of thought and even of life—*posited, that is, as anterior to every form of human relation to the world*" (9–10). In this temporality, which exceeds the discourse and practices of science and philosophy, the human subject is he who comes after in more than a temporal sense. One could instead suggest, and Friedrich Kittler has, that the subject is retrospectively inserted into "the empty slots of an obsolete discourse network [more literally, "writing system," *Aufschreibesystem*]," where he never really was, subsequently (but also matter-of-factly, indifferently), to be dismissed and killed off. ("Man simply died around 1900. It was a death to which the much-discussed death of God is a footnote.")[15] Such "experiments" have no doubt allowed—or have been shadowed by—countless exterminations as well as the survival and centrality of man, "a parade of the undead," as Tom Cohen puts it.[16]

Be that as it may, the future of that illusion may very well be at hand, although some more efforts will be required to take a fuller measure of its dissolution.[17] More soberly, it may just be the case that one merely has to wait as the rate of species extinction quickens, along with environmental devastation and the other unintended consequences of progress and profit, the work of *homo laborans*, science in action, making a buck or a living, just doing it, and all that—the increasing plausibility of what has now long been announced and actively enabled (by the nuclear bomb and other active and agentive measures). To be fair, the realm of agency has been greatly extended to include the nonhuman, but Meillassoux would most likely point out that this generalization of agents and *actants* (in the work of

Bruno Latour, for example, or even that of Donald Rumsfeld, all the way to "unknown unknowns") preserves the biases of the correlational fallacy (understandably so, since Latour emphatically, and famously, argues that "we have never been modern," neither divided nor completely disentangled—from anything really).[18] And it might be as well that we will continue to fail the Copernican revolutions as long as we persist in considering that which precedes and exceeds thought and knowledge as if it were always already related to (made, constructed, fashioned by, or co-constituted with, not to mention survived by) the human subject. Nevertheless, what I want to suggest, at the end of this extended introductory detour, is that we receive a strikingly singular kind of guidance toward exploring these matters in the subtle and wide-ranging work of Peter Szendy.[19]

## LES MOTS ET LES CHOSES

> By speaking we do not therefore so much do things with
> words as let the words "do themselves" as things.
>
> —BRANKA ARSIC, *Passive Constitutions, or 7 1/2
> Times Bartleby*

Fully committed to philosophical, musicological, literary, and rhetorical explorations (not apocalyptic ones, at least not directly), Szendy writes, he is intent on writing, a configuration of elements (and perhaps it is no con-figuration at all) that recall those evoked, if at opposite ends, by Meillassoux or Latour (and there are, of course, others).[20] He introduces us to a series of—let us call them "things," each of which "enjoins us to *track* thought" (these are often musical tracks, for Szendy, and so thought may not always be the only apparatus involved), "inviting us to discover the 'hidden passage' trodden by the latter [i.e., thought or listening, etc.] in order to achieve what modern philosophy has been telling us for the past two centuries is impossibility itself: *to get out of ourselves* [sortir de soi-même], to grasp the in-itself, to know what is whether we are or not."[21] To put it otherwise, albeit in an equally (and dangerously) abbreviated and simplified manner, Szendy transports us toward a kind of absolute ("i.e., a being whose *severance* [the original meaning of *absolutus*] and whose separateness from thought is such that it presents itself to us as non-relative to us, and hence as capable of existing whether we exist or not;" as well as "the capacity-to-be-other as such [*le pouvoir être-autre lui-même*]").[22] Such an absolute (but the world should be used in the plural, as we will see) Szendy calls repeatedly: a self, *un soi*. Every page of *Prophecies*—from the "I" to Ahab and Ishmael, from Moby Dick (the whale) to *Moby-Dick* (the book) and more—should easily confirm this.

One additional reason for this seemingly strange appellation, as he has articulated it on a recent occasion, is that Szendy also proposes a going back to Marx, and more precisely, if unexpectedly, back to Marx's early return to the things *themselves*, as it were, to the relation in and between them that "exists apart from and outside the producers."[23] Neither a positivist nor a phenomenologist (although perhaps a little bit of both, and an animist to boot), Szendy, it should be obvious, keeps rigorous watch over the terms, movements, and consequences of the Copernican revolutions we have been reviewing.[24] With Marx (and with others), he asks us to return to what constitutes yet another turn of these revolutions and indeed, as Marx knew, "a very strange thing."[25] This is the possibility that a thing—but what is a thing?—could be endowed with a *self*: nothing less, in other words, than to be *absolved of relation to the human*. Minimally and more precisely, after Marx one would have to conceive of a thing, any thing, as being endowed with a relation to self (in this case a relation of understanding—"ein selbstverständliches . . . Ding," says Marx's German—which demands that the meaning of both these words, *self* and *understanding*, be taken up otherwise, as at once more restricted and more capacious).

Walter Benjamin proposes a different, and striking, formulation. "The commodity," Benjamin writes, "wants to look itself in the face [*die Ware sucht sich selbst ins Gesicht zu sehen*]."[26] Things, or at least certain things, have a relation to themselves. More precisely, they have a relation to their "own" selves, independently of producers or consumers. (One may recall as well Benjamin's famous statement on the work of art and its receiver.[27]) A thing (a commodity, or "labor power" itself) would thus constitute a kind of "autonomous figure," endowed with a life of its own. "Marx defines it as a 'living' [*lebendige*], 'self-acting' [*sich betätigende*], 'self-objectifying' [*sich wertschaffende*]."[28]

Minimally, it would be a kind of relation that would in turn serve as a condition, in a mode of deferment or *différance*, for its rapport with other things, if independently of human agency and production.[29] And what would be found there at the very least would be, as Marx puts it, "a social relation between objects, a relation which exists *apart from and outside* the producers."[30] A thing or a commodity—a self—would thus be a relation of sorts, not a correlation, at least not one that would associate it, as that which precedes or exceeds thought, to the human subject.[31] Marx famously theorizes and struggles against this, seeking to debunk all considerations of the very things he conjures (along with other specters) as a "flight into the misty realm of religion."[32] Szendy, by contrast, wishes to hear more, minimally, to register more. In fact, Szendy's comportment toward words and things articulates a unique engagement with Marx's selves, *absolute selves*, and with the broad set of concerns that have begun to occupy us here—not only who comes *after* the subject, but indeed, what comes *apart from and outside* it? His general answer is, as I have said, a self, *un soi*, and it is one (or again, many) that could even apply to him, to his own many selves and to other selves too, as they might emerge from Meillassoux's invitation ("to *track* thought," no doubt, but mostly to *sortir de soi-même*, to get out of one's "own" selves—an ecstatic movement and a proliferation of selves) or from Melville's (who named one of his most famous and absolute selves "Moby Dick" and indeed, as Szendy brilliantly demonstrates, *Moby-Dick*). And although it follows Marx, a singular and literal reading of Marx, such an answer no doubt requires some elaboration, some explanation.

For who, or rather, *what* is a self? What kind of thing, what kinds of things, are indicated or designated by that word? *Indication* seems the adequate term to use as we set out, although it hardly brings the matter to full clarification. A self may be (or point to) an "abstract universality," but it is not a subject, much less a sovereign, nor does it necessarily *point* to an existing, *identifiable* entity, an in-dividual

even. The self (*le soi-même*) "has to be conceived outside of all sub-
stantial coinciding of self with self [*de soi avec soi*]."[33] It is nothing
personal, in other words, perhaps a type of the impersonal.[34] It is also
not human, or by no means exclusively so. More generally, a self may
be the very thing that "repels the annexations by essence," a unity in
the making, as it were, and one that lies "outside of the community
of genus and form, and does not find any rest in itself either, unquiet,
not coinciding with itself."[35] The possibility of pointing, or of identity
(to be achieved or not), may thus be contingent on something—a
relation—like a self.

Indeed, we may agree for now that, although it is not fully reducible to linguistic or rhetorical effects, "self" is or functions at the very
least as a kind of deictic (though obscure, the history of the term, its
etymology, leading up to its recent substantive turn, "*the* self," con-
firms this), and like all such shifty pointers, it oscillates between part
and whole. Is a self part of a larger whole, no more perhaps than a
former (or later) self? "I call myself an intelligence," said Kant, and
went on to suggest that that (very?) self may be understood along
the analogical lines of "an elastic ball"—the ball is a self—"that
strikes another one in a straight line [and] communicates to the later
its whole motion, hence its whole state . . . and this in turn would
share the states of all previous ones," although according to this
model "it would not have been the very same person in all these
states."[36] Is a self wholly identical—a pleonastic figure—with that to
which it nonetheless points as it turns back upon itself? Or is it an
addition, a supplement, to such a whole (a better self, as it were, at
least more aware of itself)? Or does it precede the whole of which it
is a part, like these marks that exceed, break from, and perhaps
engender their context?[37] Turn or return and ecstatic rupture (a conversion of sorts)—these are additional features of deictics and
pointers, indications that are obviously contingent (and thus hardly
self-sufficient) on a repetition that announces, constitutes, and repro-
duces, indeed, replicates and multiplies the *modus operandi* of the
deictic: here and now (and again) a self—that is not one. "In the
recurrence to oneself [*dans la récurrence à soi*] there is a going to the
hither side of oneself [*en deçà de soi*]."[38] Conversion and repetition

will also occupy us here, now and throughout, as if *automatically*. Conversion and repetition: But of what? And, precisely, toward what?

A quote from Szendy's most recent work should provide the beginnings of an illustration, with as of yet no expectation of delivering complete clarity. Still, it should illustrate. In this particular case, the thing (or object) is a song—as I have already said, Szendy is, by training and inclination, a musicologist, though the extent of his perceptive reach can hardly be reduced to music—and, more precisely, a hit song (what's more, it is a 1957 hit song whose title—theme and subject—is "Hit Song [*Le tube*]," by Boris Vian), which Szendy paradoxically puts into correlation with Marx's commodity, Marx's thing and its phantasmagorical emergence as *absolved of relations*. Better yet, in Szendy's rendering, the possibility of entering into any relation would presuppose a rapport with self that could only be described as *absolved* of any relation *except a relation to self*, which precludes oneness as it enables (and defers) identity. This would be one instance where Meillassoux's sense of the correlationality of philosophy, its betrayal of the Copernican revolutions, comes to its limit.

> What one could call the musical self or the lyrical I of the song would then be *the voice of the commodity itself, in the process of speaking about itself* [*en train de parler d'elle-même*]. For such would be the phantasmagoria at work here. . . . This musical commodity that the song is *understands itself and recognizes itself* [*se comprend ou se reconnaît elle-même*]. It enters into a relation with another, which is nothing but another version of itself, with which it exchanges itself [*avec laquelle elle s'échange*]. And those who sing or whistle the melody seem to be able to meet, to enter into a relation, only to the extent that the said melody is already busy with itself [*ledit air a déjà affaire avec lui-même*], has already understood and recognized itself.[39]

A melody—a thing or commodity—has or is a self: in this case, a musical self. Always already having a relation to itself, always "busy with itself," this singular self becomes what it is by having or gaining the capacity to transform itself in relation to itself as well as to relate to others (that is, the capacity to be related to by others). Always "in the process" of becoming itself, it always already has to have a "relation to nonpresence."[40] To the extent that it can continue to be referred to as a thing, such a thing—such a self—by no means constitutes an essence, nor perhaps ever achieves an identity. Such a self would therefore not be a subject or a sovereign (although it may become one, as it were, later in history).[41] Rather, it has (or is) a relation to itself, constituted as a differential and, more precisely, *differantial* relation.[42] This relation involves a minimal perspective, a viewpoint, as Benjamin has it, one that lets go of, indeed precedes and exceeds (later perhaps enables), a human perspective on it.[43] Akin to, but not identical with, "the self-supporting jug [that] has to gather itself for the task of containing,"[44] the thing described here has to do with a movement or pose, the business (*affaire*) of "a possible self-reflection [*une possible réflexion sur soi*]."[45] The thing is a relation to self and *therefore* a self. And let me say right away that though this might sound like anthropomorphism or personification, we should refrain from understanding it in this manner (unless one recalls that *persona* was, first of all, a thing, and would therefore have to be thought in nonanthropomorphic, nonanthropocentric terms).[46] The song is by no means a person here, nor is it "personalized." Nor is it "a statement of sameness between the researcher and the researched, but it becomes, a fortiori, an individual (yet not necessarily personal) mark of identity."[47] In other words, it might still be (that is, have a relation to) a self. What is more, the self of the song, here its voice, precedes any gesture of personification, much as it precedes the possibility for those listening to it to enter into relation with it. Its own relation to itself has, or so it would seem, *nothing to do* with its relation to others. And what this indicates, as we shall see in what follows, is essential to what Szendy presents us with, namely, a generalization and pluralization of the self—a *narcissism of the other thing*, if you will, and a notion that is therefore not one, even if it is absolute. Szendy, in other words, elaborates an unprecedented *ipsology*, and more, a *general ipsology*.

Incidentally, "unprecedented" is hardly the attribute Szendy seeks or pursues. If we are astonished to hear these self-elaborations, he goes on to explain, the reason for our reaction is "not that we hear something new (the melody is banal, the scene is as well), but rather that we are listening out of an unheard-of musical self [*depuis l'inouï d'un moi musical*] dimly perceived as if in a dream."[48] In fact, Szendy insists on banality, constantly problematizing the possibility (and value) of the new and even of the unique. For what is at issue, Szendy understands all too well, is "valid not only for the order of 'signs' and for all languages in general but moreover, beyond semio-linguistic communication, for the entire field of what philosophy would call experience, even the experience of being."[49] One could therefore speak here not only of that which exceeds and precedes thought but of any "units of iterability, which are separable from their internal and external context and also from themselves,"[50] that is, precisely of that which must remain the case for anything, any thing and indeed any "mark that subsists, one which does not exhaust itself in the moment of its inscription and which can give rise to an iteration *in the absence and beyond the presence of the empirically determined subject* who, in a given context, has emitted or produced it."[51] In other words (and specifically, Marx's words), "apart from and outside the producers." To quote Meillassoux again, we are repeatedly asked to consider "a world that is *separable* from man," earth (or at least the universe), an order or object that is "more indifferent than ever to human existence, and hence indifferent to whatever knowledge humanity might have of it," which possesses, in other words, "a power of persistence and permanence that is completely unaffected by our existence or inexistence."[52]

But let us assume, for now, that this has little to do with "thing theory," and that it is merely a linguistic, grammatical matter.[53] Let us assume that the selves—for they are many—toward which Szendy repeatedly turns his attention and ours belong to the "field of the mark," that they are "units of iterability, which are separable from their internal context and also from themselves, inasmuch as the very iterability which constituted their *identity* does not permit them ever to be a unity that is identical to itself."[54] No doubt, we are already getting ahead of ourselves, but we might still take an additional step and agree, in fact, that the question of this element Szendy calls "self [*soi*]" carries us toward, and away from, a certain sense of identity. Let us say, then, "let us say that a certain self-identity of this element (mark, sign, etc.) is required to permit its recognition and repetition."[55] It is inscribed in Szendy's language, and it can be repeated through translation and otherwise. But can it?

This is indisputably, and at least from the outset, a question of translation. As Derrida explained, a mark, any mark, must have the capacity to break from its (authorial or linguistic) context. Consider, therefore, that in order to be attributed, as it were, *back* to an author or performer (as if it did not precede or exceed that particular context), a mark must be remarked, *remarquée*. It must be noticed, obviously, but it must also be repeated and minimally repeatable. This is precisely what Szendy tries to explain about music—a field of marks if there is one, a "network of effacement and of difference, of units of iterability"—early in his very first book. I quote the original French: "C'est que la musique, pour être attribuée, doit *se remarquer*. Par exemple, dans la langue, dans les paroles, dans les *lyrics*. Pour pouvoir être signée, elle doit se doter d'une marque supplémentaire, d'une remarque."[56] The difficulty in translating this passage has to do with the self, that is to say, with the minimal inscription here of the word or particle, the mark, *se*, which unproblematically enough indicates a reflexive form, a reflexive turn or turn of phrase.[57] But along with and beyond the grammatical theology about which Nietzsche warned us, one could relate to two distinct singularities in these sentences. First, "music" is the grammatical subject. By what figure of speech or grammatical necessity does something like this happen? Or is one to consider that the sentence makes sense along with, in spite of, or against the objections of "personification" or "anthropomorphism"?[58]

The second singularity has to do more directly with the reflexive particle, which, to be semantically rigorous, would have to be preserved in the translation as significant insofar as it indicates, indeed, establishes a relationship between music and itself. Music must mark and remark itself, the sentence would (also) say. It must endow itself (*se doter*) with another mark (even if the same mark repeated) in order to be signed. But a more idiomatic (and presumably less anthropomorphizing) translation, one respectful of the idiom (or is it the self?) in and of the English language, would simply assert that there must be an additional mark made *on* music and *in* it in order for the signature to be recognized. This mark would have to be written, presumably *by* someone (or some thing?) in order for authorship to be sealed. It is easy to argue that the reflexive form of the French verbs simply corresponds to a different construction in English, one that would have to be idiomatically rendered in a passive construction (much as the process of attribution is placed in a passive form in the original French). Music, in other words, is simply not a self. And a translator's responsibility must remain that of making sense, of refraining from obscurity and obfuscation. Music does not have a relation to itself, nor does it do anything to itself, perhaps not to others, either, and certainly not by endowing "itself" with marks of any kind. *Cela*, as Szendy puts it in idiomatic French just a line or two below, *paraît aller de soi*. It seems to go without saying, which is to say, I think, that it is not a matter of self, or *soi*, but that it nonetheless does go by itself, according to itself. Unlike music, which does not. Or does it?

It seems benign enough to remind ourselves, we who would have a rapport with our selves, that music does do all kinds of things. That it has a variety of effects. To acknowledge this is hardly controversial, so long as one does not go too far and begin to attribute "agency" to music.[59] But perhaps we would have to go further, taking flight into the misty realm of religion, and claim that music— whether or not it has agency—has a rapport with self? Is this at all possible? Is not music a thing? That, again, may go without saying. But does that mean that music has a self? That it is or has a *soi* and that it has a relation to itself? Considering the risk of relating to music as an autonomous figure endowed with a self, if not with a life, of its own, entertaining relations with itself (as well as with, but this is secondary and even a matter of indifference, the human race) is quite precisely what the few French sentences I have been discussing seem to suggest. At least, that is what they could be said to say *literally*. Let me translate them accordingly: "Music, in order to be attributed, must *remark itself*. For example, in language, in its words, in its lyrics. In order to be signed [for music to be able, to have, as it were, the power, *le pouvoir*, to be signed], it [or she, *elle*] must endow itself with a supplementary mark, a re-mark."

Grammar, or at least French grammar, as I have tried to render it in less than idiomatic English, does lead us to believe (or at least to suspend disbelief with regard to the fact) that music can have a relation to itself. Prior to (or aside from) its being commodified, indeed, for it to be exposed to the possibility of commodification, it must first be exposed to that risk and seen in "a relation which exists apart from and outside the producers," in a "social relation between objects," even if that object is, for music, music itself.[60] Only in this manner can music transform itself in its relation to itself. Such is, again, *literally* the case in the original French.[61] Or perhaps, as Szendy immediately adds, this means that music has to literalize itself, or better literarize, itself. *Peut-être se littéraliser—se littérariser?* Can music transform itself into literature? Is this what is necessary to turn Marx (and a few others, including the English language in its idiomaticity) on his head? Reading Szendy in French, one might insist on maintaining, in the same language, *ça peut se lire comme ça.* It can certainly be read this way. But then, and always literally, it might also be possible for it *to read itself* this way. Belying its Cartesian reputation, French fails to bring clarity. Or maybe it's just me. I mean myself. At least in relation to a thinking self.

And you should try reading, for example, the next chapter (nay, the very first sentence!) of *Musica Practica*: "J'intitule ainsi—sous réserve—un discours qui *se* retire d'avance, comme s'il *se* ménageait la possibilité d'une mauvaise lecture, *s'*excusant d'emblée, jusqu'à *se* rendre peut-être illisible [I entitle "under reserve" (that is, until further review) a discourse that retracts *itself*, as if it were managing for *itself* the possibility of a poor reading, excusing *itself* in advance, to the point of rendering *itself* perhaps illegible]."[62]

We might have to take seriously "the extraordinary recurrence of the pronominal or reflexive, the *self* [se]—which no longer surprises us because it enters into the current flow of language in which things show *themselves* [*les choses* se *montrent*]."[63] We might also have to take seriously that what Szendy is trying to draw in flowing and rigorously stylized language constitutes the "outline of a mutation with which one would have to contend."[64] A self-transformation and the transformation of self. And indeed, one could summarize the entirety of Szendy's extraordinary work as contending, precisely, with unprecedented, which is to say, eminently repeatable mutations.[65] The notion of self that he deploys could be understood quite precisely along the lines of a "care of the self," which is to say, a relation to self and a conversion or transformation of self and to self (*convertere ad se*, as Foucault invokes it).[66] It functions, in fact, quite precisely as an account of change and mutation, an extended relation of selves, of selves relating to themselves as well as to others, such that, distinct every time, the necessary possibility of (grammatical or ritual) repetition enables or conditions, as it were internally (say, between me and myself), change and/or persistence, inasmuch, that is, "as the very iterability which constitutes their identity" does not permit them ever to be a unity that is identical to itself.[67] Within and beyond grammar, apart from and outside the producers and performers, Szendy persists in contending with the *mutation* of that which exceeds and precedes thought and thereby affects and transforms it. That is what he refers to as "selves," and he does so by considering a relation from which humans would be, if not excluded, minimally indifferent and *thereby* transformed; and before that, rendered at least contingent and derivative, effects of something that is no agency of their own, no invention, either, and yet that constitutes the very condition of possibility for agency, fashioning, creation, production, and reproduction. And their *interruption de soi*.[68]

I have begun to suggest that that relation to self, this mutation of the self, which begins with a being busy with oneself, cannot but recall the "care" or "concern" for the self (*le souci de soi*) of which Foucault speaks. It should be obvious, however, that by the time he turned to his own, renewed concerns with the matter, Foucault had collapsed the notion of the self with the notion of the subject. As Pierre Hadot, who provided much of the inspiration for Foucault's inquiry into these very matters, puts it, Foucault "is precisely focused far too much on the 'self,' or at least on a specific conception of the self."[69] Hadot points out that the Stoic, for example, does not find his joy in his "self" but rather "in the best portion of the self" (the self as part or whole). Furthermore, "joy is to be found 'in the conscience turned toward the good; in intentions which have no other object than virtue; in 'just actions.' Joy can be found in what Seneca called 'perfect reason' (that is to say, in divine reason)" (the self as supplement).[70] This suggests that the "self" in question could be found elsewhere. And as the reference to divine reason makes clear, it is hardly to be taken for granted as human, or reduced to this.[71]

Hadot concludes that "the 'best portion of oneself,' then, is in the last analysis a transcendent self. . . . In fact, the goal of Stoic exercises is to go beyond the self, and think and act in unison with universal reason."[72] This is why, "from an historical point of view, it seems difficult to accept that the philosophical practice of the Stoics and Platonists was nothing but a relationship to one's self, a culture of the self."[73] At stake was, rather, a relation to a different whole, which constituted the self as a relation of care. Indeed, for Hadot, "the feeling of belonging to a whole is an essential element: belonging, that is, both to the whole constituted by the human community, and to that constituted by the cosmic whole."[74] Clearly, "such a cosmic perspective radically transforms the feeling one has of oneself."[75] Hadot does not disagree with—he in fact insists on—the sense of transformation (conversion, mutation, and metamorphosis) that he too calls a rapport to self, a care of the self.[76] But Hadot also underscores that what is being cared for, what is being "forged," is not one's "own" individuality. Thus in the case of writing practices, for example, he deems it "incorrect to speak of 'writing of the self': not only is it not the case that one 'writes oneself' [*on ne s'écrit pas soi-même*], but what is more, it is not the case that writing constitutes the self."[77]

If there is "a movement of conversion toward the self," this is because the self is not to be identified with the human (and certainly not with the individual human). Instead, "one identifies oneself with an 'Other': nature, or universal reason, as it is present within each individual."[78] This indeed "implies a radical transformation of perspective, and contains a universalist, cosmic dimension, upon which, it seems to me, M. Foucault did not sufficiently insist. Interiorization is a *going beyond oneself*; it is universalization."[79] The disagreement between Foucault and Hadot resides, therefore, in the meaning of the term *self* and in understanding the nature of a relation to self implied by the notion of "care of the self." And though it seems unlikely that either would want to pursue a nonhuman or nonanthropocentric reading of the relation to self they both attend to, unlikely that they would ever include words and things, it is nonetheless crucial to recognize that the meaning of the notion of self remains open and contested between them, and does so precisely to the extent that it carries a sense of that which "goes beyond" the human, that which exceeds (and perhaps precedes) the human self. One example should suffice, under the heading "the metamorphosis of the self": "Then the seer no longer sees his object, for in that instant he no longer distinguishes himself from it; he no longer has the impression of two separate things, but *he has, in a sense, become another.* He is no longer himself, nor does he belong to himself, but he is one with the One, as the centre of one circle coincides with the centre of another."[80]

There is something else. Hadot, and Foucault after him, are both in agreement as to the "spiritual" nature of the relation—or rather, relations—to self they seek to document and retrieve. Foucault (who by now appears to have fully identified self and subject, as Hadot rightly pointed out) seems to show some hesitation, as if to underscore the arbitrariness of the term *spiritual.* Having agreed "to call 'philosophy' the form of thought that asks what it is that enables the subject to have access to the truth and which attempts to determine the conditions and limits of the subject's access to the truth," Foucault goes on with the following proposition: "If we call this 'philosophy,' then I think we could call 'spirituality' the search, practice, and experience through which the subject carries out the necessary transformations on himself in order to have access to the truth." Does this mean that we could call this something else? Could we, for example, consider this search and these transformations as instances of what Marcel Mauss called "techniques du corps"?[81] Surely the term would be available to the thinker of "techniques du soi" and kinds of "practical schema" toward a transformation of the self.[82] Foucault does seem to open the possibility that these and other terms are plausible enough, but the opening closes before any such possibility materializes. Instead, having just proposed that we adopt the term, he promptly decides to enter (in the very next sentence) into an unproblematic rapport with himself, a rapport of agreement and, indeed, self-affirmation: "We will call 'spirituality' then the set of these researches, practices, and experiences, which may be purifications, ascetic exercises, renunciations, conversions of looking, modifications of existence, etc."[83]

Hadot, for his part, engages in a longer conversation with himself ("the practice of dialogue with oneself" having been held in high regard as a "spiritual exercise") in order to determine how to characterize the practices and exercises he too agrees (with himself) to call "spiritual."[84] In fact, Hadot goes further than Foucault in asserting that "it is . . . *necessary* to use this term."[85] Why? Because to suggest that these might be "intellectual" exercises or practices of "thought" would not do justice to all that is involved (something that apparently does not include the "flesh"). Is it not the case that such insistence on the spiritual may recall a Christian history, even though the reference is to practices that precede Christianity? Does this not recall a "conception of religion" that is "a modern, privatized Christian one because and to the extent that it emphasizes the priority of belief as a state of mind rather than as constituting activity in the world"?[86] Hadot seems to treat such an objection as a historical problem rather than as a conceptual (much less a theological) one.[87] Spirit it is, even if Philo of Alexandria enumerates, among such spiritual exercises, bodily practices such as reading, listening, and "indifference to indifferent things."[88] It is not for me to interrogate the spiritual meaning and intent, the psychic thrust even, of these exercises. But I do want to register the recurrence of a certain prejudice against matters of the flesh. More importantly, and since we are talking about the meaning of the self in its human and inhuman dimensions, we might consider that "the care of the self" seems to imply a relation to self that is not exhausted by its spiritual nature, that it indeed "entailed practical forms of behavior" and other bodily matters.[89] The transformation of vision and of listening (a concern that is at the center of Szendy's work) involves precisely material and bodily selves. It also involves musical selves, "phantom limbs (or members)" and, beyond them, machines and instruments and other works, other selves. With them, with Szendy, we remain within the larger problematic of a rapport to self as that which challenges and decenters—because it exceeds and/or precedes any human subject—the humanism of narcissism. It is therefore time for us to turn toward the narcissism of the other thing, the logic of other selves.

## AUTOPHONY

Beginning in fact with *listening*, which will slowly and indirectly bring us closer to *reading* (the two constituting in fact his most compelling departure points), Szendy wonders at one point whether anything new has occurred in the history (more precisely, the history of our ears) he traces.[90] The specific moment is the appearance of the DJ and of his instruments (primarily the phonograph, which, incidentally, preceded the DJ). With them, Szendy writes, "another era of listening *may* be beginning," an era, he continues, "which I don't know what to call."[91]

If such is the case, if something new or different is beginning, it is because of a new kind of self, a musical self, one that would fail to sustain the distinction between "production, reproduction, and reception."[92] With the DJs, "who are essentially doing nothing different from what I do in my listening room," the difference between these three attributes becomes "confused." What is thereby redefined is, however, not just a different relation to music, which the English translation of *Listen: A History of Our Ears* faithfully renders. For if DJs are us, if they are performing the same gestures we do when we listen, it is "because they are simply *listeners appearing in concert.*" Once again, though, the French text adds an idiomatic, reflexive particle, which signals toward a becoming that reflects back on that which we are, on the kind of listening self that we are: *des auditeurs se produisant en concert.* And here again it is difficult to ignore not only the temporality of the passive activity being described ("where production, reproduction, and reception tend to be *confused*"), through which we ourselves *become* the auditors we are, but also that in exposing ourselves, in appearing and producing ourselves in concert, we are, in fact, *producing ourselves* as listeners. We are becoming listeners, at once making ourselves *into* listeners and *transforming* ourselves. Whether or not this is in fact our own doing, it seems clear that not only our relation to music would be changing as we listen, but our relation to ourselves as well, to selves that, strictly speaking, did not exist prior to their production.

And there is yet another turn: if we want to understand the relation of this self to itself, the term *production* cannot quite be maintained without remainder. For this is, let me repeat myself once again, "where production, reproduction, and reception tend to be confused." No wonder that such selves can absorb things "often without realizing it—to the point of sometimes themselves transforming [*jusqu'à se transformer parfois eux-mêmes*]" into listeners or judges (72). This is all very human, so far, all too human. Sometimes, though, as a well-versed music lover once recognized, "the melodies themselves undergo the strangest metamorphoses."[93] And sometimes too, an instrument suddenly acquires a self, seems at least to transform itself and its self into one.

In this particular case—it was literally one brought before a court—the possibility that a machine might take the witness stand also opened the image of an unprecedented figure of speech, a prosopopoeia. Brought to court by "an obscure individual by the name of Vives," Edison's phonograph "changed drastically the liberal legal concepts that, until around 1900, left the field wide open for makers of mechanical instruments."[94] But the agency of these instrument makers is not what interests Szendy most directly here. Rather, he is concerned with the transformative nature of the phonograph, as well as with the "fascinating prosopopoeia" through which "it is indeed the phonograph, a *speaking* instrument that takes the stand here and *testifies for itself*."[95] The French makes clear that it is indeed the phonograph "itself" that "takes a hold of speech [*qui prend ici la parole*]" and, again, "testifies for *itself* [*témoigne pour* lui-même]." "The commodity itself is the speaker here."[96] But is the phonograph, this massively transformative instrument, to be considered a self? That is, of course, what the figure of prosopopoeia does, attributing a voice to that which is inanimate. "At the bar, the phonograph speaks and says 'I say that I speak.'"[97] And yet it would be inaccurate to claim to have found here more than what the figure literally brings about: a figurative instance of self. Still, what are we to make—if making is what is here required—of the transformative power of the machine and beyond it of this new invention called phonography? For "the fact is that, beginning with this affair, phonography, *insofar as it spoke*, became a publication."[98]

Thus was born the modern record in its juridical status. Its ability to speak, though, not to mention its ability to transform the world around it ("this was a revelation for the Court," writes Vives), cannot be exhausted by the figurative *attribution* of a voice to an inanimate object. Indeed, the object does speak and more: it inaugurates "the era of the reproducibility of *all* possible sonorities, human and non-human."[99] The voice is not attributed to it.[100] It is, rather, the phonograph, and with it phonography, that speaks. Literally so. Doing so, it speaks for itself and about itself ("I say that I speak") and must be considered a nonanthropomorphic entity endowed with a relation to self, if only by virtue of repetition and reproduction. It must be clear, however, that this is another instance "where production, reproduction, and reception tend to be confused," which is what begins to explain the inscription of a self in and as "thing." It is a nonhuman self, no doubt, and this is precisely what is significant. And for now, it will suffice to consider that this self is not the presupposed agent that the machine would "be" as it acts on others. Rather, the self is that which is produced by the machine, as the machine, insofar as it takes the stand and takes hold of speech.

But "the disappropriating power of mechanization" would soon participate in the further literalization of such figures.[101] "It will be for us a matter of listening; we will literally hear in it our ears being fabricated [*nous y entendrons littéralement se fabriquer notre oreille*]."[102] In listening, our very own ear has begun to have a relationship to itself. It is making a self for itself, making itself. And beyond music—a matter of translation—we will have to ask about the iteration of such selves, appearing as if by way of citation. Can an image too, not only a song or a sound, have a relation to itself? "Is there truly, when it comes to quotation, a *structural* difference between music and the plastic arts or cinema, for example? In other words: could an image, *in itself* [en elle-même] show that it is a quotation, without any recourse to a text, a title, a signature, a caption?"[103]

Before following the lead of other selves, it seems important to recall that when it comes to listening, and to its fashioning, Szendy is also attending to the contingencies of reception and perception. We might return to Szendy's own version of "the reader in the text," but for now let us note that he is looking for the listener in the work by questioning the historicity of the notion of work in music as well as by interrogating the metamorphoses of our ears. "The making, *la facture*, of the modern ear" is how he refers to it, an "organology of our ears," in which "it becomes more difficult than ever to distinguish between *the organ* and *the instrument*."[104] Rather than affirm the agency of the listener, his organicity or instrumentality, yet without dismissing any of these, Szendy simply pursues other selves. Music, Szendy argues, or at least some *pieces* of music, offer or articulate—speaking perhaps figuratively—figures of listening, *des figures de l'écoute*.[105] Doing so (and we have begun to see that this may not be a doing at all, at least not exclusively so), in these particular instances, music, music itself, would "constitute a form of self-reflection [*une forme d'autoréflexion*]."[106] And this form (of the self in its relation to itself) would be cited, as it were, repeated again and again elsewhere—repetition being of the essence. In the concert hall, for example.

> The public concert, ever since it came into being, has been in effect a kind of mirror of listeners. It is not just a place to hear works. It is also a theater where the members of the public observe each other. And themselves [*un théâtre où le public s'observe. Lui-même*]. It is a space where we come to look at those who listen. Where we go to see people listening, or even to listen to people listening [*voire pour écouter écouter*].[107]

The difficulty of a translation increases the difficulty of distributing agency, defining the boundaries between activity and passivity, even if it enables with no uncertainty the identification of selves, and their multiplication. Listening itself appears to be listening, to itself, as we, listeners, become what we are, listeners, as we listen to ourselves (and to each other) listening to self-reflexive figures of listening. Somehow "listening to (oneself) listening [*(S')écouter écouter*]" sediments the sense of a self (and more precisely, of selves) which easily precedes and exceeds a human history.[108] "Rather, we should view this history, for which I have gathered scattered bits and pieces and various accounts, as a complex, stratified process, involving different *speeds of sedimentation*."[109] Furthermore, "the listening in question here is not that of a given listener, or of a category of listeners one has to *take into account*; it is rather *structural listening* in Adorno's sense—or even beyond Adorno, a listening *without listener* in which *the work listens to itself* [*une écoute* sans auditeur *dans laquelle* l'oeuvre s'écoute]."[110] We will soon be "confronted with other mutations" and with the "plasticity" of such selves, a "generalized plasticity" that would repeat and cite a generalized ipsology.[111] "We have tracked down the moments of this *reflexive return to self* [*les moments de ce retour réflexif sur soi*]," here is a self, then, absolved of all relations, for now, except a relation to self. Here is listening's plasticity, from which a self—an I—emerges.

> *To listen to oneself listening* [S'écouter écouter] (if that were possible) . . . to fold listening onto itself and onto oneself, isn't that also risking not hearing anything anymore of what is available to be heard, isn't that *becoming deaf*? It is in the space of this risk that I ask you a few final questions: about the *responsibility of listening*; and about its *plasticity*.
>
> To listen to oneself listening. . . . It is, in any case, this improbable reflexivity that dogs my listening, that holds it in its attention. The listener I am [*l'auditeur que je suis*] is nothing, does not exist as long as you are not there. There or elsewhere, it doesn't matter, so long as my listening is addressed to you. The listener I am [*je suis*] can happen only when I follow you [*je te suis*], when I pursue you.[112]

## OTHER SELVES

We have only begun to consider the multiplication of "these similar unities, substitutable, moreover (indeed, infinitely figurative [*tropiques*]) that are fingers, feet, organs, in short, the *members* of this 'society' called body. Or 'self.' "[113]

It might be necessary, therefore, to draw up a preliminary count, a body count or an account of the selves that populate Szendy's body of work. Only by doing so will we be able to contend with their figurative (or tropic) status, keeping in mind that the genealogy (*filiation*) linking them to the human body, to the body said to be proper (*corps dit "propre"*) derives its "beauty, its force no doubt from its organicist and anthropo-centered presupposition: we, we-men, would have given birth to instruments-spaces," selves of one sort or another, "which would be extensions of our body and of our organs, with complex ramifications, yes, but with no solution of continuity."[114] The force and beauty of a genealogy that sees in selves anthropocentric projections testifies to the ultimate anthropocentrism, in other words, the correlative assumption that *only* human (or living) beings could be endowed with a self.[115]

The entirety of the proper/figurative distinction sustained by this presupposition is nowhere near collapsing, and yet without a "solution of continuity," Szendy seems to push us toward the abolition, indeed, the *absolution* of our anthropocentric, collateral, prejudice. The possibility of considering the possibility of a relation to self (of bodies, instruments, organs, or works, and more generally things, commodified or not) that would precede or exceed a human hand, human touch, perception, or cognition appears lacking in Western organology. It constitutes no more than a kind of monstrosity, at best a source of curiosity.

> Yet if Western organology has seen no more than curiosity [in such bodies], it is perhaps because it was unable or unwilling to see the law, in truth, the only *model* available for thinking its own project: a kinship of sonorous bodies *amongst themselves*, their genealogies in which the body said to be "human" ("my" body) would be no more than a particular case, if a remarkable one. It is possible, therefore that, in the final count . . . organology was not able to come to terms and break with an anthropocentered logic of the evolution of bodies.[116]

It might also be important to mention that the bodies of which Szendy writes here, while asking us to renounce our anthropocentric logic, are all endowed with the attribute of property: a relation of self to self, as proper *to* itself, which the Greeks called *idios*.[117] This is not to renege on the movement of disappropriation mentioned earlier, but rather to recall that the tropes of the self (and perhaps, if this helps, the self as a trope) involve a double movement. Its "identity" is "paradoxically the division or dissociation of itself," while its unity "only constitutes itself by virtue of its iterability, by the possibility of its being repeated."[118] That is why Szendy can affirm the existence of a listening he calls (in English) "split-hearing," the

possibility of "a listening that would bear *within itself* its own disso-
nance, its unresolved duplicity, its fission not absorbed into fusion."[119]
To the extent that there is such a thing as listening itself, a self of
listening, it would always already be a *double agent*.[120]

Surely, there are selves other than "musical selves" in Szendy's
work (though one should keep in mind that this appellation includes
instruments and melodies, bodies and body parts of musicians and
machines). There are texts, whose relation to themselves is one of
writing or reading.[121] There are individuals, of course (some of
whom we have already encountered, but a few more are coming up),
and there are collectives too, themselves proliferations of "bodies that
are closed and detached entities, the unity of which is *in itself* prob-
lematical [*dont l'unité est* en soi *problématique*]."[122] There is the question of how they (individual and collective selves) come together by
way of an *animation* and a *conduction*, that of the conductor, whose
actions consist in "making noise behind oneself [*faire du bruit derrière
soi*]," something that raises all kinds of questions as to the kinds of
political selves implied by the notion of *actio in distans* and implicates
magnetism, dynamism, and, well, despotism.[123] There are intimations of *possessions* and *hauntings*, whereby one self is taken over by
another—human or inhuman. (Rameau's nephew is said to have a
body "only to the precise extent that he first lets himself be possessed
[*il se laisse d'abord posséder*] by other bodies."[124] There are intimations
of becoming not so much who one is, in other words, but becoming
a self one may never have been, and yet, still and for the first time, a
self of sorts. We have seen in the preceding pages that a whale, or a
book, is or has a rapport with self that implicates other selves at the
same time as it remains indifferent to them, indifferent at least (and
again) to human selves.

Throughout, it is as if we were constantly reading "une allégorie
du son en tant qu'il s'écoute," an allegory of self and sound insofar
as it is listened to; insofar and primarily as it listens to itself.[125] And
indeed, we have begun to witness the "infinite affirmation of self"
of the song, whereby the song appears to "play itself or by itself," to
"play with itself," and even to "laugh at itself." (The French phrase
is "la chanson se joue d'elle-même.")The song appears to dig into
itself an ironic distance "from itself to itself [*de soi à soi*]," something

that transforms it into an allegory of self or of itself.[126] Szendy himself suggests that such a self cannot but be registered as *tautegorical*.
"It says nothing other than itself . . . it explains itself."[127] The self of
a song—and not only haunting songs that *possess* to the point of
exhaustion the entirety of a self—would thus be "its own musicol-
ogy," its own mythology even, something that would bring it at once
closer to and further from "myth" as the ultimate *tautegory* described
by Jean-Luc Nancy.[128] Why closer? Because endowed with the same
formal properties, but further too because testifying to *a general ipsology*, the self of a song (and the song as self), perhaps the self as such
(if there were such a thing in this proliferation of selves) would be
one of those "intimate anthems that seem to function as a gathering
of a subject to itself [*un ralliement du sujet à soi*], to itself as unique
and singular."[129]

Still, it will come as no surprise that the first self that inscribes
and repeats itself in (and on) Szendy's texts is the I. "I'm listening
[*J'écoute*]," begins *Listen*; "I am here [*je suis là*]," continues *Membres
fantômes*; "am I heard or listened to? [*suis-je écouté?*]," asks *Surécoute*.
And one would hardly force the self of these texts by asking about
the status of the "I" that speaks these lines (rather than all too quickly
restrict it to the inscription of an authorial voice, for example). In
many ways, I myself have been asking (myself, I think) nothing else
throughout. "Je suis une écoute," volunteers unforgivably (for a
translator, at least) a voice close to Kakfa in *Surécoute*.[130] As Nietzsche, quoted early on in *Membres fantômes*, knew well, "always the
self listens and seeks: it compares, compels, conquers, destroys. It
rules and is also the rule of the ego."[131] The self, Szendy promptly
explains, cannot be confined to the human. It can be seen in (or
behind) musical organs, bodies or instruments. Granted, there are
cases when it might be found behind an "I," but it is not to be
confused for all that with the psychoanalytic unconscious. It is a self
vis-à-vis which one must renounce deciphering a pulsional body or
an "it speaks [*ça parle*]."[132] We are still looking, in other words, for a
word or a way of translating this self. And if music lends a helping
hand; if music is, as we have seen, "a manner of saying *oneself* [*une
façon de* se *dire*]" that "puts into play the unity of self [*qui met en jeu
l'unité de soi*]," it is because music itself raises the possibility of a

formal parallel whereby "the bound, the organic unity (of music and of self) can only be conceived on the background of relays, substitutions and displacements," and therefore with the multiplication of selves.[133] Beyond music, such a self might have everything to do with the repetition and the play of an "I" (*le jeu d'un "je"*),[134] but it could be that the I or self of organs and instruments, of sounds and bodies, of *membra disjecta*, is exponentially multiplied (*démultipliés*), like the fingers or feet of a well-trained and mutated pianist, objects and instruments affected by a general condition of *autophonie autoreproductrice*, whereby "bodies of changing and uncertain virtualities expose themselves [*les corps sonores s'exposent*]," affirmed or undermined in "the autocratic confidence and the affirmation of self [*l'autocratique confiance et affirmation de soi*]" that sustain them.[135] This, at least, is what Szendy explicitly explores in *Membres fantômes* and elsewhere, uncovering stranger selves yet, such as a contraption, an "automembranophone without musician," that seems to sound and resound without reason all on its own; an entropy of bodies, "a manner of disseminating the soul [*une manière de diffuser l'âme*]," of transforming and multiplying bodies. A "specific un-binding [*déliaison*] of bodies," a "vast process of un-binding" these "members of the 'society' named body. Or 'self' [*'soi'*]."[136]

ISOLATES

"What is identity," Jacques Derrida asks, "this concept of which the transparent identity to itself is always dogmatically presupposed by so many debates . . . and before the identity of the subject, what is ipseity?" Ipseity, which precedes (and perhaps exceeds) the subject, is what, following Szendy, I have been referring to as "self." Derrida makes clear that ipseity "is not reducible to an abstract capacity to say 'I,' which it will always have preceded."[137] One could therefore suggest that a self does not have to speak or, alternatively, that speaking is only one form of the relation to self that goes, and more frequently does not go, under the name of self. Derrida elaborates when he writes of:

> some automobilic and autonomic turn or, rather, return to self,
> toward the self and upon the self . . . some quasi-circular return or

rotation toward the self, toward the origin itself, toward and upon the self of the origin . . . the autonomy of the self, of the *ipse*, namely, of the one-self that gives itself its own law, of autofinality, autotely, self-relation as being in view of the self, beginning by the self with the end of self in view—so many figures and movements that I will call from now on, to save time and speak quickly, to speak in round terms, *ipseity* in general.[138]

The self is engaged, it is articulated, and better, constituted as and through "a complicated set of relations," all of which are (as we read in Derrida's words, and as we have been seeing and hearing in Szendy's work) first and foremost forms of a relation to self. Among these forms, Derrida underscores the importance of "possession, property, and power,"[139] which have also occupied us, but we have considered that there may be others. Be that as it may, and understandably so, the general ipseity of which Derrida writes seems to call for a general ipsology, a field of research of sorts that would include the human self, of course, but also question the humanist prejudice and go beyond it, toward words and things, as well as toward the self implied in the viewpoint of the commodity (as Szendy has it after Benjamin). In these cases and beyond them, under the heading of self, in other words, what a general ipsology would try to approximate and to circumscribe would indeed be a circularity, a turn or return that is absolved of relation to a human subject. And so we have indeed been considering what would be "a world that is *separable* from man" and "more indifferent than ever to human existence, and hence indifferent to whatever knowledge humanity might have of it," a power indeed, as Derrida insists, and minimally "a power of persistence and permanence that is completely unaffected by our existence or inexistence."[140] We have been considering, Szendy tells and shows us, that we are reading after, and perhaps past, Melville.

Melville's "delineation of individuals" is well known:

who, because of birth or achievement or action or character—a white jacket of some kind, in short—were set apart from normal human relationships. These persons may appropriately be called "Isolatoes," a term coined by Melville himself in describing the crew of the Pequod: "They were nearly all Islanders. . . . 'Isolatoes' too, I call such, not acknowledging the common continent of men, but each *Isolato* living on a separate continent of his own."[141]

The matter, as Szendy formulates it, has to do with sociability ("What would there be, *at bottom*, between you and me, that would make of each of us, not peninsulas (I cannot manage to see a continent), but atolls or reefs emerging from a subaquatic architecture?").[142] Yet within "the abyss I imagine lying between our insularities," it is always already a question of ipsology: "Would we be mobile islets, then, monadic enclosures adrift in the midst of a vast ocean, on or under the undulating surface from which run Leviathan-texts that swell until they seem to comprehend everything?"[143] This interrogation carries with it a range of selves, whether "I's" or books or whales (each of whom joins Ishmael in declaring "meditative transcendence of the self," or what Szendy calls *retroprospective* reading, as their aim).[144] Minimally, it means to contend seriously with the possibility "that the book, this very book (*Moby-Dick*) is written *on* the whale, as a subject or a theme. But equally leviathanic is the text to the extent that, like the whale, it encloses and contains all. It welcomes all. . . . it is a world in the world."[145]

The entirety of *Prophecies*, and perhaps of Szendy's work, could thus be summarized in the following sentence: "Slowly, something is going to happen to 'I.'"[146] Although it should be noted that the translation once again cannot avoid failing the letter of Szendy's prose. It is the letter "I," of course, that he is discussing, insofar as something occurs, something happens to it. But the sentence says something more: "Quelque chose, lentement, va arriver à 'je.'" Which also means that something will arrive, something will reach or approach (the place of) an "I," transform "itself" into an I, in relation to an I that is nothing but this relation. The rapport to self we have been pursuing with Szendy articulates, therefore, a temporal relation, what Jacques Derrida calls a "relation to nonpresence."[147] A self then, not necessarily human, you recall, perhaps even a storm, "would be but an enclosure of time: an event already included and framed between its anticipation of itself and its consecutiveness upon itself [*un événement déjà inclus entre son anticipation sur soi et sa consécu-tion sur soi*]."[148] Absolved of relations ("The beast is here alone. It enters into a ménage with no other"), it is therefore no wonder that the self is in need of "a stake or a prop, its erection and its settlement within its sovereign identity to itself."[149] But what happens, then, to the I? "Or rather: What will happen if I, if the eye of the text, opens (and opens itself) to what or who comes to inscribe and carve in his hearth and home a *center of intrusion*?"[150] To the extent that there could be a general ipsology, it could never be about the self as such, but always already about "self-interruption," more precisely, its in-terruption of self (*interruption de soi*), an "unceasing self-interruption [*autointerruption*]" to the point of "self-tearing [*autodéchirure*]."[151] Does the self (or the text) "lose its own self-possession [*sa possession de soi*]"?[152] Finding oneself, finding oneself reduced to oneself, might mean precisely to encounter this self as a "contradictory movement, "tossed about between a tightening and a loosening, between con-traction and expansion, as if there were playing within [the self] a terrible and simultaneous counterpoint of attachment and ultimate detachment."[153] Commenting on Kierkegaard elsewhere, Szendy ex-plains that access to the self (*l'accès à soi*):

> to the most singular in, and to the most hidden of, the self is con-tingent on the absolutely banal [*l'absolument quelconque*]. It opens itself—if it opens itself—in the experience of banality . . . this *access* is at once a passage and, according to another dimension of the word, a *crisis*. Access to self and access *of* self (as one would say of an access of fever [or an access of rage]). The I which is subject of and subject to such access . . . this I endures . . . a trial of self [*l'épreuve de soi*].[154]

As Melville himself describes it in *Moby-Dick*, prophesying a differ-ent scenario for Freud's "oceanic feeling": "The intense concentra-tion of self in the middle of such a heartless immensity, my God! Who can tell it?"(93:414).

Who, then, speaks (of, to, or for, and as) a self? Does the self speak? Must it? Is the attribution of a self to music and to language, to bodies, machines, and instruments, to words and things as well as to beasts and texts, merely a mechanical (perhaps even the *automatic*) repetition of the well-known figure of prosopopoeia? Are these selves, which we have encountered and not encountered—to which we have had *access*—in "a congregation of atoms properly *isolated*," are these selves still human, all too human? Are they our own doing and making, our inventing and fashioning selves, reaching and expanding into the world, recognizing ourselves as we relate to that which will never be absolute, never absolved of human relations, but precisely co-relational? Szendy is relentless in arguing not so much *otherwise* as simply *selfwise*. But things are, of course, far from simple. It is worth repeating (indeed, it is worth repeating, and rereading, the far from simple selves of Peter Szendy). Or perhaps—*cela va de soi*—it goes and repeats itself: "a voice comes out of its muteness and speaks through the text: through this immense prosthetic and prophetic mask that, like a strange and monstrous *persona*, masks nothing but itself."[155]

# NOTES

PREFACE TO THE ENGLISH-LANGUAGE EDITION: READING
AND THE RIGHT TO DEATH

1. The opportunity for such a rereading was granted me recently by Richard
Rand, whom I would like to thank here. With his typical subtlety and careful-
ness, he indicated to me a few mistakes in the French version of *Prophecies*. I
had wanted to translate myself the passages from *Moby-Dick* that I cite, since
Jean Giono's translation (the only one available at the time) is more or less
useless, as I explain a number of times. Armel Guerne's 1954 translation had
been out of print until it was finally republished in 2005, whereas the faithful,
if less creative, version by Philippe Jaworski was supposed to be published only
in 2006, in the La Pléiade collection. As Rand explained to me, I had simply
mistranslated the lines I comment on at the beginning of the chapter entitled
"Backfire." Fortunately, this error of translation is without consequence for
the argument I am trying to elaborate. Moreover, since one does not translate
a translation, the English-language reader of *Prophecies*, who reads Melville in
the original, will know nothing about it. Why, then, do I point out here that
one note was corrected, in which I discuss Guerne's proposed translation of
this passage? It is because my error of translation (as well as Guerne's) is no
doubt a symptom: what was at stake for me, in interpreting these so very
difficult lines, was the sovereignty *of the text*, insofar as it is "unconditional"
and "integral." I cannot reconstitute the entirety of Rand's brilliant demonstration as he reconstructed the chain of occurrences of this signifier ("integral")
in Melville's novel. I do hope Rand will let us read one day his unique way of
reading Melville's oeuvre, as he has begun to do in a recent article ("Melville
et l'Amérique," in *Po&sie* 120). However, I can and must say that the present
preface to my *Prophecies* is an attempt to elaborate anew, out of an error, this
question of the sovereignty of the text. Which is to say, of its life and of its
death.

2. I cite from the standard modern English edition, John Donne, *Biathanatos*, ed. Michael Rudick and M. Pabst Battin (New York: Garland Publishing, 1982).

3. John of Salisbury, *Policraticus. Of the Frivolities of Courtiers and the Footprints of Philosophers*, trans. Cary J. Nederman (Cambridge: Cambridge University Press, 1990), 6.

4. On *effictio* and the reinterpretation I propose of this ancient figure, see my *Membres fantômes: Des corps musiciens* (Paris: Minuit, 2002), to be published in Richard Rand's translation by Fordham University Press.

5. This is what Pierre-Emmanuel Dauzat suggests in his introduction to the French edition (Paris: Presses Universitaires de France, 2001), 14, referring to the second treatise by John of Apamea ("he crucified himself"; in *Dialogues et traités* [Paris: Cerf, 1984], 152). In Donne's treatise, the term *biathanatos*, whence the title, appears only once (in the eighth section of distinction 6 of part 2), to designate "persons reputed viciously to have killed themselves" (138). The word is a late Greek neologism, used to refer, particularly in Chrysostom, to "he who dies a violent death." Later the term acquired the martyrological sense of "suicide," as in Tertullian's *De Anima* (56n8 and 57n3).

6. [Like the English *meteorism*, the French word *météorisme*, obviously linked to the meteoric and meteorological concerns that Szendy explores throughout *Prophecies*, designates physiological symptoms such as bloating, the "distension of the abdomen, esp. by gas in the gastrointestinal tract or peritoneal cavity" (*O.E.D.*).—Trans.]

7. Werner Hamacher has attended to these Christological echoes in the later corpus of Hegel in *pleroma—Reading in Hegel* (Stanford: Stanford University Press, 1998).

## PROPHECIES OF LEVIATHAN: READING PAST MELVILLE

1. [Between the insistence on deferral (postponement) and the posting of bills, the posting of sentinels, that of captains and of "little King-Post," as well as the postal logic of destinations and predestinations never reached—prophecies (never) accomplished—the word *poster* seemed here a better occasion, a better translation, and a more fitting word for this announcement of what is (what was and will be) to come in Szendy's unposting (that is to say, unhurried) reading of prophecy. This explains why, when possible, I have translated the word *envoi* (an insistent Derridean echo in Szendy's prose) by "posting," it being understood that the slightly more accurate "sending" would have also suffered much-deserved criticism. Cf. Jacques Derrida, *The Post Card: From Socrates to Freud and Beyond*, trans. Alan Bass (Chicago: University of Chicago Press, 1987), and see Bass's exquisite translator glossary, esp. *envoi* (xx–xxi) and

*poste* (xxv–xxvi). Only that which is posted can be read, yet once posted it is also past reading, beyond it: a constant risk, and above all for the translator. Hence, "Reading Past Melville" for *Lire selon Melville.*—Trans.]

2. [Although he consistently refers to the English original, Szendy relies on the French translation by Lucien Jacques, Joan Smith, and Jean Giono (Paris: Gallimard, 1941), if only to modify it or to highlight, as he writes in the notes to the original French edition, "the needs of a reading to the letter."—Trans.]

3. Quoted in Charles Olson, *Call Me Ishmael* (San Francisco: City Lights, 1947), 39.

4. Herman Melville, "I and My Chimney" in *The Piazza Tales and Other Prose Pieces, 1839–1860*, (Evanston, Ill.: Northwestern University Press, 1987), 352.

5. Sovereignty, writes Jean-Luc Nancy in "Ex nihilo summum," is "not . . . the quality of being at the summit but the summit itself," the one "whose being consists in height" (*The Creation of the World, or Globalization*, trans. and introd. François Raffoul and David Pettigrew [Albany: State University of New York Press, 2007], 96).

6. William Shakespeare, *King Lear*, 3.1.1. It seems that Melville was particularly marked by his reading of *Lear*. Charles Olson reports that "it was *Lear* that had the deep creative impact" (Olson, *Call Me Ishmael*, 47). In Melville's copy, "this play is marked more heavily than any of the others" (48).

7. The Latin word *aura*, "breath, wind," yielded the Old French *ore*, "breeze," whence derives *orage*, "thunderstorm." But one also finds, in the lexicon of nineteenth- century psychology, the *hysterical aura* or the *epileptic aura* to name some sensations that *precede the attack*. The great *Larousse* of the nineteenth century thus gives for *hysterical aura*: "Peculiar sensation of a vapor that seems to rise from the body toward the head, prior to a hysterical attack. . . . The *aura hysterica* is the sensation of a *ball* that, starting from the hypogastrium, according to some, from the epigastrium, according to others, rises slowly to the throat, where it provokes either aphonia or dysphasia and produces a spasm of the glottis, which immediately precedes the convulsive movements of hysteria."

8. "Aqueous meteors," one reads in the article "Météore" in the *Encyclopédie* of Diderot and D'Alembert, "are composed of vapors, or aqueous particles. Such are clouds, rainbows, hail, snow, rain, dew and other similar phenomena." One also speaks of *hydrometeors*.

9. See Kings I, 16:29ff.

10. "Météoromancie," in Diderot and D'Alembert, *Encyclopédie*.

11. According to the conventions of international meteorological observatories, twenty-one letters are used, from *A* to *W*, but never *Q* or *U* (not enough first names begin with those letters, it seems). Here is the complete list of these

first supernames [*surprénoms*], each waiting for its turn and return: Alberto, Allison, Arthur, Ana, Alex, Arlene, Beryl, Barry, Bertha, Bill, Bonnie, Bret, Chris, Chantal, Cristobal, Claudette, Charley, Cindy, Debby, Dean, Dolly, Danny, Danielle, Dennis, Ernesto, Erin, Edward, Erika, Earl, Emily, Florence, Felix, Fay, Fabian, Frances, Franklin, Gordon, Gabrielle, Gustav, Grace, Gaston, Gert, Helen, Humberto, Hannah, Henry, Hermine, Harvey, Isaac, Iris, Isidore, Isabel, Ivan, Irene, Joyce, Jerry, Josephine, Juan, Jean, José, Keith, Karen, Kyle, Kate, Karl, Katrina, Leslie, Lorenzo, Lilly, Larry, Lisa, Lee, Michael, Michelle, Marco, Mindy, Matthew, Maria, Nadine, Noel, Nana, Nicholas, Nicole, Nate, Oscar, Olga, Omar, Odette, Otto, Ophelia, Patty, Pablo, Paloma, Peter, Paula, Philippe, Rafael, Rebecca, René, Rose, Richard, Rita, Sandy, Sebastian, Sally, Sam, Sherry, Stan, Tony, Tanya, Teddy, Teresa, Tomas, Tammy, Valerie, Van, Vicky, Victor, Virginia, Vince, William, Wendy, Wilfred, Wanda, Walter, Wilma.

12. It is true that some selection is often made, since the most violent storms are usually taken off the lists. Too many victims, too much damage, a bad *name*: Luis, Marilyn, Opal, and Roxanne were too murderous in 1995 and have been replaced for 2001 by Lorenzo, Michelle, Olga, and Rebecca. Andrew devastated Florida in 1992, so Alex took his place for 1998. In 1998, George retired for the benefit of Gaston for 2004.

13. Cicero, *De Divinatione*, trans. William Armistead Falconer (Cambridge: Harvard University Press, 1923), 1.14.24; trans. modified.

14. Ibid., 1.18.34.

15. "The Lightning-Rod Man" was on pp. 131–34, the *Israel Potter* installment on pp. 135–46; cf. Mark Niemeyer, "Narrative Thunder; or, the Double Axes of Poetic Romanticism in 'The Lightning-Rod Man,'" in *The Piazza Tales: Herman Melville*, ed. Bruno Monfort (Paris: Armand Colin, 2002), 119.

16. An example of this form of "linguistic stammer" is found in the French word *grenouille* ("frog"), which derives from the Latin *ranucula* (diminutive form of *rana*) by way of addition—which is to say, prosthesis—of the letter *G*.

17. Maurice Blanchot, "Prophetic Speech," in *The Book to Come*, trans. Charlotte Mandel (Stanford: Stanford University Press, 2003), 79.

18. *Pierre, or The Ambiguities* is without a doubt the Melville novel most explicitly dedicated to premonitions and prophecies of all kinds. There, Melville even appears to allude to the practice of meteoromancy: "In their precise tracing-outs and subtile causations, the strongest and fieriest emotions of life defy all analytical insight. We see the cloud, and feel its bolt; but meteorology only idly essays a critical scrutiny as to how that cloud became charged, and how this bolt so stuns" (Melville, *Pierre, or the Ambiguities* [Evanston, Ill.: Northwestern University Press, 1971], 4:67).

19. Ibid., 3:43; emphasis added.

20. Quoted in Olson, *Call Me Ishmael*, 109.

21. I leave aside here the case of Benjamin Franklin and his lightning rod, which relates both to Noah (insofar as it protects with foresight against the thunderstorm) and to Ahab (who defies the sky by tying it to the earth, as I will show below).

22. [The French expression "se faire un sang d'encre" means "to worry exceedingly." Literally, it refers to a blood that would be as dark as ink.—Trans.]

23. I register here only two among the multiple occurrences of Jonah in the novel. In chapter 75, speaking of the whale's "mouth," Ishmael cries out: "Good Lord! Is this the road that Jonah went?" (75:334). Then, in chapter 102, announcing that he is about to describe the skeleton of the sperm whale *from the inside*, Ishmael addresses a few false objections to himself, in the following terms: "But how now, Ishmael? How is it, that you, a mere oarsman in the fishery, pretend to know aught about the subterranean parts of the whale? . . . A veritable witness have you hitherto been, Ishmael; but have a care how you seize the privilege of Jonah alone" (102:448).

2.4 [The French here is "comme un corset par des baleines." Like the "ribs" of an umbrella, the stay of a corset is, in French, referred to as its *baleines*, literally, its "whales."

25. Jean Giono's translation simply ignores this last sentence, leaving it untranslated.

26. In "Bartleby, or On Contingency," Giorgio Agamben dedicates a few pages to a beautiful analysis of these "dead letters" as "the cipher of joyous events that could have been, but never took place" (Agamben, *Potentialities: Collected Essays in Philosophy*, ed. and trans. Daniel Heller-Roazen [Stanford: Stanford University Press, 1999], 269).

27. Hawthorne added the *W* to his name in order to untie it from this past of sinister memory—even if, and not without irony, this letter is the initial of the word *witch*.

28. The text of the "Return" was printed by Increase Mather as an appendix to his *Cases of Conscience Concerning Evil Spirits Personating Men, Witchcrafts, Infallible Proofs of Guilt in Such as are Accursed with That Crime* (Boston: Benjamin Harris, 1693).

29. See the interesting debate published in *The New York Review of Books* 26, no. 4 (March 22, 1979), in response to an article by Edmund S. Morgan, "The Puritan You Love to Hate," in the same journal (25, nos. 21–22 [January 25,1979]).

30. I. Mather, *Cases of Conscience*, 67.

31. "Learned men give it as a most certain sign of possession, when the Afflicted party can see and hear that which no one else can discern any thing

of, and when they can discover secret things past, or future, as a possessed person in Germany foretold the War which broke out in the year 1546" (ibid., 40–41).

32. The evidence provided by the victims of witchcraft, insofar as it comes from afflicted individuals, "is not meer humane Testimony. And if it be in any part Diabolical, it is not to be owned as Authentick. For the Devils Testimony ought not to be received neither in whole, nor in part" (ibid., 49).

33. This is what Increase Mather suggests when he writes that "a free and Voluntary Confession of the Crime made by the Person Suspected and Accused after Examination, is a sufficient ground of Conviction" (ibid., 59).

34. Hannah Arendt, *On Revolution* (Harmondsworth, Middlesex: Penguin Books, 1990), 82–88.

35. Ibid., 106–7, see also 293n42: "Although the etymological root of *persona* seems to derive from *per-zonare*, from the Greek *zōné*, and hence to mean originally 'disguise,' one is tempted to believe that the word carried for Latin ears the significance of *per-sonare*, 'to sound through.'"

36. I borrow the term *hauntology* from Jacques Derrida, in his *Specters of Marx: The State of the Debt, the Work of Mourning, and the New International,* trans. Peggy Kamuf (New York: Routledge, 1994), 10.

37. In his translation, Armel Guerne translates partially (and, I think, wrongly), inserting the I instead of "life" as the disputant (*Moby Dick ou Le cachalot blanc*, trans. Arnel Guerne [Paris: Le Sagittaire, 1954], 838). As for Giono, he simply does not translate. The problem lies, of course, in the abrupt and seemingly contradictory juxtaposition of two adjectives qualifying mastery: "unconditional, unintegral." Must one add a "but" (as I would be wont to do) between them, to make the paradox explicit? Obviously, behind the difficulty of translation there is hidden, perhaps, something else: an aporetic thought of sovereignty (of life)?

38. Guerne translates "unsuffusing" with *inétendu*, "without extension," but this is a bit remote. "To suffuse" means "to saturate," "to fill," "to engorge," "to permeate and imbue," speaking, for example, of a color on a cloth or of a liquid. (Giono, true to form, once again avoids the problem.)

39. "At rows of blank-looking counters sat rows of blank-looking girls, with blank, white folders in their blank hands, all blankly folding blank paper" (TM, 328).

40. "The history of the political is a history of paper, if not a paper history," says Derrida in *Paper Machine*, trans. Rachel Bowlby (Stanford: Stanford University Press, 2005) 61.

41. Before the sentence cited by Melville (who misleadingly identifies it as the *incipit* of *Leviathan*, as the "opening sentence of Hobbes' Leviathan"), before these words, which you have just read, Hobbes, in fact, writes (and these are the very first sentences of the book):

Nature (the Art whereby God hath made and governes the World) is by the *Art* of man, as in many other things, so in this also imitated, that it can make an Artificial Animal. For seeing life is but a motion of Limbs, the beginning whereof is in some principall part within; why may we not say, that all *Automata* (Engines that move themselves by spring and wheeles as doth a watch) have an artificiall life?" (Thomas Hobbes, *Leviathan*, ed. Richard Tuck [Cambridge: Cambridge University Press, 1996], 9)

Thus, the Leviathan-State is presented as a giant automaton, an artificial man-animal-machine, whose members or parts are "natural" men: "The *Magistrates* . . . artificiall *Joynts*," "*Counsellors* . . . are the *Memory*," and so forth (ibid.).

42. As Carl Schmitt writes, in Hobbes's work "the leviathan signifies the state and the behemoth represents revolution." (*Behemoth*, the title of another work by Hobbes, published after his death in 1682, is, according to Schmitt "a symbol of the anarchy brought about by the religious fanaticism and sectarianism that destroyed the English commonwealth during the Puritan Revolution.") Leviathan and Behemoth are tightly related, so it is true that for Hobbes the State is nothing but "civil war which can only be prevented by overarching might." Thus, everything is as if "one of the monsters, the leviathan 'state,' continuously holds down the other monster, the behemoth 'revolutionary people'" (Schmitt, *The Leviathan in the State Theory of Thomas Hobbes*, trans. George Schwab and Erna Hilfstein [Westport, Conn.: Greenwood Press, 1996], 21).

43. Cf. Etienne Balibar's preface to Carl Schmitt, *Le Léviathan dans la doctrine de l'État de Thomas Hobbes* (Paris: Seuil, 2002), 64n65.

44. Ibid.

45. Hobbes, *Leviathan*, 11.

46. Ishmael's question ("What am I that I should essay to hook the nose of this Leviathan!") is a parody or a paraphrase of Job 41:1–2, where God asks Job: "Can you draw out Leviathan with a hook? . . . Can you put a hook into his nose?" Here one could broach a kind of spectral dialogue between Melville and Schmitt. The latter did, in fact, retrospectively try to attenuate his involvement in the Third Reich by arguing, in a manuscript fly sheet signed "Benito Cereno," that his study of Hobbes was a "coded critique of Nazism" (cited in Wolfgang Palaver's Afterword to the French edition of Schmitt's *Leviathan*, 221). See Carl Schmitt, *Le Léviathan dans la doctrine de l'État de Thomas Hobbes: Sens et échec d'un symbole politique*, trans.Denis Trierweiler (Paris: Seuil, 2002). Schmitt seems to have identified (or thought he could) with the title character of Melville's "Benito Cereno," the apparent captain of a ship

that is actually governed by rebelling slaves. Schmitt concludes his 1938 book with a drawing that in the original edition of Schmitt's book also figured on the cover. As Palaver shows, this illustration reproduced by Schmitt is itself a response to Hobbes and his engraver's great frontispiece (219). It is borrowed from illustrations accompanying the medieval tradition, which interpreted Leviathan as the devil, baited by Christ and caught by God by means of the cross as hook. In Schmitt's rendition, however, one only sees Leviathan half washed up on land, with a hook coming out of its mouth and attached to nothing . . .

47. Cf. chapter 18 of *Leviathan*, where Hobbes explains that, for the common good, men must "appoint one Man, or Assembly of men, to beare their Person; and every one to owne, and acknowledge himselfe to be the Author of whatsoever he that so beareth their Person, shall Act, or cause to be Acted, in those things which concerne the Common Peace and Safetie. . . . This is more than Consent, or Concord; it is a reall Unitie of them all, in one and the same Person, made by Covenant of every man with every man. . . . This done, the Multitude so united in one Person, is called a COMMON-WEALTH, in latine CIVITAS. This is the generation of that great LEVIATHAN" (Hobbes, *Leviathan*, 120).

48. Melville, "I and My Chimney," 353, 356.

AFTERWORD: IPSOLOGY (SELVES OF PETER SZENDY), BY GIL ANIDJAR

1. Quentin Meillassoux, *After Finitude: An Essay on the Necessity of Contingency*, trans. Ray Brassier (London: Continuum, 2008), 121; further references will be made in the text. It should already be apparent that by "Copernican revolution" Meillassoux is not referring to Kant's self-proclaimed turn (see note 6, below). Neither did Freud, for that matter, who omitted Kant from his own list: Copernicus (decentering the earth in the cosmic order), Darwin (decentering the human being in the natural order), and Freud himself (decentering the ego in the psychic and social order).

2. As Emmanuel Levinas puts it, "subjectivity qua knowing is thus subordinated to the sense of objectivity [*la subjectivité en tant que savoir se subordonne donc au sens de l'objectivité*]" (Levinas, *Otherwise than Being, or Beyond Essence*, trans. Alphonso Lingis [Pittsburgh: Duquesne University Press, 1998], 132).

3. "An abyss opens up where a bridge should have been built and, if some connections are woven . . . they also appear in the paradoxical figure of disconnection [*déliaison*] or, as Heidegger would say, of absolution" (Philippe Lacoue-Labarthe and Jean-Luc Nancy, *The Literary Absolute: The Theory of Literature in German Romanticism*, trans. Philip Barnard and Cheryl Lester [Albany: State University of New York Press, 1988] 30).

4. Hannah Arendt, *The Human Condition* (Chicago: University of Chicago Press, 1998), 1.

5. Alan Weisman, *The World Without Us* (New York: Thomas Dunne, 2007). This mean that it will not be possible to ignore the "politics of survival" at work implicitly or explicitly, here and elsewhere (including, perhaps, in the pages that follow), so eloquently described and criticized by Elias Canetti in *Crowds and Power*, whereby one "wants to live longer than everyone else, and to *know* it," to know what happens *after* and witness not only the end of the world but, and no less paradoxically, its aftermath (Canetti, *Crowds and Power*, trans. Carol Stewart [New York: Farrar, Straus and Giroux, 1984], 227). Equally pertinent is what Martin Harries describes, in a wonderful book, as "fantasies of modern spectatorship" articulating "the threat of, or the desire for, an experience of spectatorship so overwhelming that it destroys the spectator" (Harries, *Forgetting Lot's Wife: On Destructive Spectatorship* [New York: Fordham University Press, 2007], 14–15).

6. As is well known, Kant describes his critical project as analogous to that of Copernicus, although he does so in terms that produce a recentering in the knowing subject (rather than the decentering of that subject). Kant writes: "Hence let us once try whether we do not get farther with the problem of metaphysics by assuming that the objects must conform to our cognition, which would agree better with the requested possibility of an *a priori* cognition of them, which is to establish something about objects before they are given to us. This would be just like the first thoughts of Copernicus, who, when he did not make good progress in the explanation of the celestial motions if he assumed that the entire celestial host revolves around the observer, tried to see if he might not have greater success if he made the observer revolve and left the stars at rest" (Immanuel Kant, *Critique of Pure Reason*, trans. and ed. Paul Guyer and Allen W. Wood [Cambridge: Cambridge University Press, 1998], 110 [B xvi]).

7. Lacoue-Labarthe and Nancy describe the Kantian turn in comparable terms when they write of its "systematic programming" as finding its authority in "a positing of the world itself as a correlate [*corrélat*] of the subject," even if, for Kant, this subject is not yet a laboring and productive one. Production and creation, "the *work* of the subject," were soon to become coextensive with the subject. Cf. Lacoue-Labarthe and Nancy, *Literary Absolute*, 33.

8. See G. B. Vico, *The New Science*, trans. Thomas Goddard Bergin and Max Harold Fisch (Ithaca, N.Y.: Cornell University Press, 1968); on Descartes, I was fortunate to hear a paper in which Samuel Weber restores the agency (and the agitation) at work in Descartes' *cogito*. Examining the semantics of the word, Weber reads Descartes (or at least his word) as carrying out a kind of thinking with, indeed, a doing with (Weber, "Climate Change: The Question of Prognosticating," University of Albany, SUNY, April 2007). Charles

Taylor expresses the general investment in laboring and productive agency when he recalls "the etymological link [made by Augustine] between '*cogitare*' and '*cogere*' = 'to bring together' or 'to collect.' This understanding of thinking as a kind of inner assembly of an order we construct will be put to a revolutionary new use by Descartes" (Taylor, *Sources of the Self: The Making of the Modern Identity* [Cambridge: Harvard University Press, 1989], 141).

9. Michel Foucault, *The Order of Things: An Archaeology of the Human Sciences* (New York: Vintage Books, 1994), 387.

10. An almost comical rendering of Freud's assertion about the decentering of the human subject is quoted by Barbara Johnson from *The New York Times*, which attributes agency to man all the way down (like turtles, perhaps): "From Copernicus pushing us from the center of the universe to Darwin tying us to the lowliest of life forms, *man has routed himself* from his place of relative importance in the cosmos" (quoted in Johnson, *Persons and Things* [Cambridge: Harvard University Press, 2008], 154; emphasis added). Freud is, obviously, omitted from this account.

11. "Ab-solution," which Levinas also invokes, corresponds in fact to an "undoing [of] all the structures of correlation" (Levinas, *Otherwise than Being*, 148; and see, e.g., 49–50). Levinas insists on the structures common to self, signification, and the other, arguing that "subjectivity is imposed as an absolute" (59). These terms, as in Meillassoux, cannot be subsumed under the heading of "correlationism" but must instead be understood as "outside of every system, before any correlation" (70), "outside of everything" (86), "without a context . . . coming from the emptiness of space, from space signifying emptiness" (91), "outside of any correlation and any finality" (96), and, finally, as "a nonrelation, but absolutely a term," one that is "not reducible to a relation, but yet is in recurrence" (103). But Levinas's formulations are perhaps most familiar with regard to the other who exceeds being as well as the capacities and categories of knowledge, who comes outside of any contextual relation. Meillassoux's absolute might also be found in the striking descriptions of Christian Jambet (commenting on the Islamic philosopher Mulla Sadra) as a *world*. "The idea of 'world,'" explains Jambet, "is the idea of an absolute totality, such that there is nothing external to it. Consequently, a 'world' has no place. Understood correctly, the 'world' is perfect and complete in itself and, consequently, has neither a 'where' nor a 'place.'" It is absolved of relations (Jambet, *The Act of Being: The Philosophy of Revelation in Mulla Sadra*, trans. Jeff Fort [New York: Zone Books, 2006], 37).

12. Meillassoux refers to a larger project in which he hopes "to develop the theoretical positions that we are merely sketching here, as well as their ethical consequences: *L'inexistence divine: Essai sur le dieu virtuel [Divine Inexistence: An Essay on the Virtual God]*"(Meillassoux, *After Finitude*, 132n15). In a personal communication, Meillassoux kindly referred me to the fascinating work

of Graham Harman, who elaborates an "object-oriented philosophy" after and against Heidegger (Graham Harman, *Tool-Being: Heidegger and the Metaphysics of Objects* [Chicago: Open Court, 2001]). Unfortunately, space is lacking here to do justice to the numerous and pertinent points of resonance between Harman and Szendy and to their philosophical rigor, but I will mention that what Harman advocates is a version of the absolute, indeed, a restoration of "a necessary concept of substance," where "an entity always holds something in reserve beyond any of its relations" (230), except perhaps for the Levinasian "relation between the entity and its being" (240). Such an entity is described by Harman as "a 'black box,' a simple integral unit that conceals an inferno of numerous interior powers and relations—forces *utterly indifferent to any human 'use' of them*" (243; emphasis added).

13. "Contrary to what is often claimed," Meillassoux explains, "the end of Ptolemaic astronomy does not mean that humanity felt itself humiliated because it could no longer think of itself as occupying the center of the world. . . . The successive upheavals brought about by the mathematization of nature are better understood as resulting from the loss of every privileged point of view and from the dissolution of the ontological hierarchization of places. Humanity becomes unable to invest the world with the meaning that had hitherto allowed it to inhabit its environment—the world can do without humanity" (Meillassoux, *After Finitude*, 136n1).

14. Eduardo Cadava, Peter Connor, and Jean-Luc Nancy, eds., *Who Comes After the Subject?* (New York: Routledge, 1991).

15. Friedrich Kittler, *Discourse Networks 1800/1900*, trans. Michael Metter, with Chris Cullens (Stanford: Stanford University Press, 1990), 4, 258. Derrida, who accompanies Szendy in his work and in his dreams, and who will accompany us throughout, explains this according to the logic of the supplement: "the *for-itself* would be an *in-the-place-of-itself*: put *for itself* instead of itself. The strange structure of the supplement appears here: by delayed reaction, a possibility produces that to which it is said to be added on" (Derrida, *Speech and Phenomena and Other Essays on Husserl's Theory of Signs*, trans. David Wood [Evanston, Ill.: Northwestern University Press, 1973], 89).

16. Tom Cohen, *Anti-Mimesis: From Plato to Hitchcock* (Cambridge: Cambridge University Press, 1994), 2; cf. Kittler's historicization: "In 1900 speaking and hearing, writing and reading were put to the test as isolated functions, without any subject or thought as their shadowy supports" (Kittler, *Discourse Networks*, 214, and further: "Every medium that brings the hidden to the light of day and forces the past to speak contributes, by gathering evidence, to the death of Man"; 286).

17. There is no hint of such dissolution in Charles Taylor's *Sources of the Self*. He straightwardly contains the issue ("We talk about a human being

as a 'self'), while immediately acknowledging that "the word is used in all sorts of ways" (32). Later on, Taylor grants as "probable" that every language has "resources for self-reference and descriptions of reflexive thought, action, attitude" (113), presumably involving humans and nonhumans, although Taylor does not say. He does warn, somewhat strenuously, against confusion between these other languages and what is presumably *the* language of modernity, for what those offer "is *not at all the same* as making 'self' into a noun, preceded by a definite or indefinite article, speaking of 'the' self, or 'a' self." Taylor clarifies, in case it was not understood, that "this reflects something important which is peculiar to our modern sense of agency" (ibid.; emphasis added). The grammatical—and anthropological—requirements for crossing the border of "our modern sense" (which is "not at all the same" as anything else) are even clearer.

18. But Rumsfeld was, of course, correct in affirming a correlation to agents he himself had much to do with. On a more serious note (as if America's wars were not serious enough), much could be made of a comparison of Latour and Meillassoux, especially of their conceptions of the Copernican revolution. For Latour, Kant is in fact *faithful* to Copernicus, "Things-in-themselves become inaccessible while, symmetrically, the transcendental subject becomes infinitely remote from the world" (Latour, *We Have Never Been Modern*, trans. Catherine Porter [Cambridge: Harvard University Press, 1993], 56). This separation, "the great split" (57), only increases with Hegelian dialectics and with phenomenology. That is why Latour advocates precisely what Meillassoux laments, namely, "a Copernican Counter-revolution" (76ff.). Latour's "Middle Kingdom" (79) and his notions of "quasi-subjects" and "quasi-objects," of "hybrids" and a "population of actants" are unmistakably instances of "correlation." Even if "silent things" are made into actors, in other words, it is all done "for the same anthropological reason" (83). (See also Latour, "Why Has Critique Run Out of Steam? From Matters of Fact to Matters of Concern," *Critical Inquiry* 30 [Winter 2004]: esp. 242.) After Meillassoux, one could maintain that ANT (Actor-Network-Theory) is a humanism. There are parallel debates among psychoanalysts (and philosophers), as Judith Butler shows in *Giving an Account of Oneself* (New York: Fordham University Press, 2005), 75–77.

19. In what follows, I have the good, if precarious, fortune to seek to provide, if not quite the rudiments of a context, indications toward the beginnings of a reading of Peter Szendy's work. This is by no means an exhaustive introduction, but it touches upon most of the books Szendy has published since the recent beginnings of his prolific career, less than ten years ago, as a philosopher, literary critic, and, of course, musicologist. Acutely sensitive to the numerous languages he knows, Szendy is also a translator (Adorno, Bartók), as

well as a regular contributor to major French publications (*Libération*, *Vacarme*), and there are other selves. I confine myself to the books except when necessary. They are, in chronological order (and with my approximate translation of their titles) *Musica practica: Arrangements et phonographies de Monteverdi à James Brown* (Paris: L'Harmattan, 1997); *Écoute: Une histoire de nos oreilles* (Paris: Minuit, 2001); translated by Charlotte Mandell as *Listen: A History of Our Ears* (New York: Fordham University Press, 2008); *Membres fantômes: Des corps musiciens* [Phantom Limbs/Spectral Members: Of Musician Bodies] (Paris: Minuit, 2002); *Les prophéties du texte-léviathan: Lire selon Melville* (Paris: Minuit, 2004); *Surécoute: Esthétique de l'espionnage* [Tapped/Overhearing: An Aesthetics of Spying] (Paris: Minuit, 2007); *Tubes: La philosophie dans le Juke-Box* [Hits: Philosophy in the Juke-Box] (Paris: Minuit, 2008).

20. Interestingly enough, the possibility is inscribed in the work of Latour's former colleague Michel Callon, who advocates an approach that "goes beyond human minds and deploys all the materialities comprising the sociotechnical *agencements* that constitute the world in which these agents are plunged," that "leaves open the possibility of events that might refute, or even happen independently of, what humans believe or think" (Callon, "What Does It Mean to Say That Economics Is Performative?" in *Do Economists Make Markets? On the Performativity of Economics*, ed. Donald McKenzie, Fabian Muniesa, and Lucia Siu [Princeton: Princeton University Press, 2007], 323), and later, "the human being is not a starting point" (346). Such events, other worlds that Callon elsewhere describes with terms such as "opacity, integrity and impenetrability" and phrases like "'I' am not the 'I' that you want 'me' to be," might be called, after Szendy, other selves (M. Callon and V. Rabeharisoa, "Gino's Lesson on Humanity: Genetics, Mutual Entanglements and the Sociologist's Role," in *Economy and Society* 33, no. 1 [February 2004]: 23, 24).

21. Meillassoux, *After Finitude*, 27; Derrida long ago pointed out that a self—or an I—in its signifying function "does not depend on the life of the speaking subject. Whether or not perception accompanies the statement about perception, whether or not life as self-presence accompanies the uttering of the *I*, is quite indifferent with regard to the functioning of meaning" (Derrida, *Speech and Phenomena*, 96).

22. Meillassoux, *After Finitude*, 28, 56; once again, though, it might be important to note that Meillassoux's emphasis on thought and knowledge (on science, in other words) could be expanded by way of a Vichian accent on making, producing, and laboring. With Szendy, it will be a matter of *sortir de soi-même* (literally, getting out of the selfsame) by *registering*—listening, recording, reading—the absolute.

23. Karl Marx, *Capital*, vol. 1, trans. Ben Fowkes (London: Penguin Books, 1976), 165 ("The Fetishism of the Commodity and Its Secret").

24. Barbara Johnson also shows that Marx is unavoidable here, and she returns to him (and to Benjamin) as well (Johnson, *Persons and Things*, 20–23, 138–43). She further asserts that "it is simply irresistible to imagine the social life of commodities without people" (22), but she herself, over against Marx, resists and does not succumb to that irresistible temptation.

25. Marx, *Capital*, 1:163.

26. Walter Benjamin, "Central Park," in *The Writer of Modern Life: Essays on Charles Baudelaire*, trans. Edmund Jephcott and Howard Eiland (Cambridge: Harvard University Press, 2006), 148; quoted in Szendy, *Tubes*, 21n7.

27. "No poem is intended for the reader, no picture for the beholder, no symphony for the listener" is how Benjamin puts it in "The Task of the Translator," trans. Harry Zohn, in Benjamin, *Illuminations*, ed. Hannah Arendt (New York: Schocken Books, 1968), 69.

28. I quote from Chris Bracken's ingenious and vastly pertinent study, and from his reading of Marx in particular, in Christopher Bracken, *Magical Criticism: The Recourse of Savage Philosophy* (Chicago: University of Chicago Press, 2007), 158; as Bracken puts it, commenting on Benjamin (and Benjamin on Marx), "the critic does not come to know the object from the outside but discovers what it already knows about itself on the inside" (147). This is comparable but hardly identical to what Arjun Appadurai calls "methodological fetishism," which suspends the view that "human actors encode things with significance" and returns "our attention to the things themselves" (Appadurai, "Introduction: Commodities and the Politics of Value," in *The Social Life of Things: Commodities in Cultural Perspective*, ed. A. Appadurai [Cambridge: Cambridge University Press, 1986], 5).

29. In Derrida's formulation, this relation would occur "from a self-proximity, an *ownness* (*Eigenheit*), which is not a simple inside but rather the intimate possibility of a relation to a beyond and to an outside in general" (Derrida, *Speech and Phenomena*, 22). In other contexts, one may speak of this relation in terms of communication (Derrida does so in *Limited Inc*), as well as exchange and circulation.

30. Marx, *Capital*, 1:163–65 ("The Fetishism of the Commodity and Its Secret"); quoted in Szendy, *Tubes*, 20; see also Bracken, *Magical Criticism*, esp. chap. 4 ("Commodity Totemism"), as well as Michael Taussig, *Mimesis and Alterity: A Particular History of the Senses* (New York: Routledge, 1993). Whereas Appadurai affirms this move away "from the exclusive preoccupation with the 'product,' 'production,' and the original or dominant intention of the 'producer,'" suggesting that "exchange" might be a more fruitful venue (Appadurai, *Social Life of Things*, 9), Taussig offers "sympathetic magic"— savage philosophy, as Bracken has it—as an alternative to the form of correlationism called "constructivism."

31. It should be clear that as brilliantly instructive (and relevant) as Barbara Johnson's inquiries are, they remain strictly within the terms of "correlationism." As she writes, "the question of things turns out to be a question of things *for people*" (Johnson, *Persons and Things*, 229). Earlier in the book, Johnson raises a different possibility, one that, as I have suggested above, she does not quite engage even if it is irresistible. "Whereas treating a thing like a man locates it in a human world, treating a man like a thing locates human beings in the realm of the inhuman. There could be something sobering and lucid about this realm, but it is never welcomed" (21). In this realm—if it is one— things would have selves, and selves would be things; every "I" would have to be "read as a prosthetic 'I'" (David Wills, *Prosthesis* [Stanford: Stanford University Press, 1995], 19).

32. Barbara Johnson lingers over the way "animation, for Marx, is always a delusion" and how he is "intent on stamping out false animation." Johnson also points out that Marx himself ends up "animating the commodities by means of prosopopoeia" while refusing to entertain and, indeed, "lust after the magic of things" (Johnson, *Persons and Things*, 140). It is this very ambivalence that makes Marx, in Chris Bracken's phrase, a "savage philosopher."

33. Levinas, *Otherwise than Being*, 114.

34. Branka Arsic beautifully considers the relation between Melville's "isolatos," the problem of the absolute, "types of the impersonal," and the way "Ishmael's problem becomes how to leave that failed contrivance called 'self'" (Arsic, *Passive Constitutions or 7½ Times Bartleby* [Stanford: Stanford University Press, 2007], esp. 85–87; see also Arsic's account of "originals," 6ff., or "mono-beings," 158). Later on, Arsic raises the Deleuzian possibility of "a disappropriated thinking, a thought that does not belong to a self" (102). One might say that Szendy explores a self that does not belong to thought or a thought.

35. Levinas, *Otherwise than Being*, 8. "The problem of any discordance between subject and self" is a necessary point of departure here (see Johnson, *Persons and Things*, 51), which does not mean that Hegel's rhetoric of self (*ansich* and *für-sich*, in-itself and for-itself) can be ignored, of course. But it might be suspended for now, by way of Levinas as well as Meillassoux's critique of correlationism (suspending as well the question of that critique's success, whatever this might mean). My purpose, as should become obvious, is not to situate Szendy within the Hegelian or anti-Hegelian tradition (I take it he has a place in both), but to consider the singular way in which selves—not subjects or substances—are deployed throughout his work.

36. Kant, *Critique of Pure Reason*, 260 [B158], 423n [A364].

37. Derrida, "Signature Event Context," trans. Samuel Weber and Jeffrey Mehlman, in *Limited Inc* (Evanston, Ill.: Northwestern University Press, 1988), 9

38. Levinas, *Otherwise than Being*, 114.

39. Szendy, *Tubes*, 21; emphases added.

40. Derrida, *Speech and Phenomena*, 65.

41. As Szendy puts it, as he displaces the self from any sovereign point of view, "there isn't, for me as a listener, a 'place of the king' [Foucault]: my position is in no way 'sovereign'" (Szendy, *Tubes*, 68).

42. "The very movement of difference," Derrida explains, implies that any "form" of presence (beginning—or not—with a self) "be infinitely repeatable, that its re-turn, as a return of the same, is necessary *ad infinitum* and is inscribed in presence itself" (Derrida, *Speech and Phenomena*, 67). The very "condition" of "self-presence," Derrida continues, must "be conceived anew on the basis now of difference within auto-affection" (68). "This movement of differance is not something that happens to a transcendental subject; it produces a subject. Auto-affection is not a modality of experience that characterizes a being that would already be itself (*autos*). It produces sameness as self-relation within self-difference; it produces sameness as the nonidentical" (82). It should be obvious that what Derrida says here of the subject and elsewhere of the trace is and must be generalized as the condition of possibility of any "self," whether human or not.

43. Walter Benjamin, "The Paris of the Second Empire" in *The Writer of Modern Life*, 88; quoted in Szendy, *Tubes*, 21. The "loss of every privileged point of view" and the "dissolution of the ontological hierarchization of places" described by Meillassoux entails a dissemination of viewpoints—a proliferation of selves—that Szendy, after Benjamin, rigorously investigates. Mick Taussig, another "savage philosopher" of Benjaminian persuasion, pertinently points out how it dawned at some point on the subject of humanism that "the native's point of view is endless and myriad" (Taussig, *Mimesis and Alterity*, 238).

44. Martin Heidegger, "The Thing," trans. Albert Hofstadter, in *Poetry, Language, Thought* (New York: Harper & Row, 1975), 168.

45. Szendy, *Tubes*, 21n7.

46. See *Prophecies*, "Spectral Evidence," where Szendy comments on the matter of *persona* by way of Arendt (*Prophecies*, 74); Barbara Johnson reviews this and other proximate figures that relate "persons and things" (Johnson, *Persons and Things*, esp. 6–18, 188–207). One could also launch a charge of animism, explicitly discussed by Szendy in *Membres fantômes*, 111ff. The most compelling discussion of this charge (which is complex and elaborate, overdetermined, in fact) can be found in Bracken's *Magical Criticism*, which deploys a Benjaminian sensibility close to Szendy's. As Bracken puts it, "magical criticism actualizes the work's own self-conscious, self-reflective life force: 'the subject of reflection is, at bottom, the artistic entity itself'" (17; quoting Benjamin).

47. I quote from Neni Panourgiá's fascinating engagement with auto-anthropology in *Fragments of Death, Fables of Identity: An Athenian Anthropography* (Madison: University of Wisconsin Press, 1995), 9.

48. Szendy, *Tubes*, 22.

49. Derrida, "Signature Event Context," 9.

50. Ibid., 10.

51. Ibid., 9.

52. Meillassoux, *After Finitude*, 115–16.

53. On "thing theory," see Bill Brown, ed., *Things*, special issue, *Critical Inquiry* 28, no. 1 (Autumn 2001). Brown explains that "the story of objects asserting themselves as things . . . is the story of a changed relation to the human subject and thus the story of how the thing really names less an object than a particular subject object relation" (4). To keep with the noncorrelational imperative Meillassoux calls for, however, we might have to follow a different path. It would begin with an undoing of the distinction between subject and object, and perhaps with a generalized ipsology.

54. Derrida, "Signature Event Context," 10.

55. Ibid.

56. Szendy, *Musica practica*, 18.

57. "Does telling oneself [*se dire*] amount to being said [*être dit*]?" asks Levinas. "The reflexive pronoun *oneself* [se] and the recurrence it denotes raise a problem; they cannot be understood solely on the basis of the said" (Levinas, *Otherwise than Being*, 43; trans. modified).

58. Bracken attributes "the canonical statement of the personification principle" to Hume, who is recycling Vico: "There is an universal tendency among mankind to conceive all beings like themselves, and to transfer to every object, those qualities, with which they are familiarly acquainted, and of which they are intimately conscious" (quoted in Bracken, *Magical Criticism*, 72; Bracken goes on to consider Nietzsche's contradictory stance on animism and the attribution of "ego" to beings and things, 77–78). As Bracken points out in his advocacy of "savage philosophy," the humankind here referred to is both "savage" and "primitive." And the contradictions of "civilized" philosophy, Bracken demonstrates, are worth exploring. Szendy's singular brand of "magical criticism" would rank, I think, quite high on Bracken's list of ancient and modern savage philosophers.

59. Or attribute agency to literature or film, two realms of particular interest for Szendy. But let me quote Steven Shaviro, who, referring to André Bazin's notion of "the instrumentality of a nonliving agent" (the camera, for example), describes how "reality is not preserved and sustained so much as it is *altered* by the very fact of passive, literal reproduction—or what could better be called hypermimetic simulation" (Shaviro, *The Cinematic Body* [Minneapolis: University of Minnesota Press, 1993], 18). As well, "to be photographed is

to be transformed" (212). For Shaviro, cinema is not conducive to identification; it undoes the self or, better yet, *subjects* it—masochistically. And disseminates it.

60. Marx, *Capital*, 1:165; see also Meillassoux, who insists that "instead of construing the absence of reason inherent in everything as a limit that thought encounters in its search for the ultimate reason, we must understand that this absence of reason *is*, and can *only* be the *ultimate* property of the entity. We must convert facticity into the real property whereby everything and every world *is* without reason, and is thereby *capable of actually becoming otherwise without reason*" (Meillassoux, *After Finitude*, 53). This conversion (the word is absent in the French at this particular moment, yet is invoked a page earlier under the heading of a *conversion du regard*—translated as "a change in outlook") should resonate both with the Benjaminian viewpoint and with the Foucauldian conversion to which I return below. Note that, when writing of Monteverdi's music (in *Orfeo*), which sounds and resounds, and listens to itself, Szendy evokes the figure of "absolute listening [*une écoute absolue*]" (Szendy, *Tubes*, 94).

61. It is, of course, no accident—and, furthermore, of multilayered relevance—that Derrida's sentence "La voix s'entend" was translated as "the voice is heard" and not as "the voice hears itself" or "the voice is heard (by itself)" (as, indeed, it appears to, by its lonesome *self*), and this in the midst of an extended reflection on auto-affection ("the subject does not have to pass forth beyond himself to be immediately affected by his expressive activity" and, a few lines below, "the phenomenon of speech, the phenomenological voice, *gives itself out* [se donne] in this manner"; Derrida, *Speech and Phenomena*, 76).

62. Szendy, *Musica Practica*, 25; emphases added.

63. Levinas, *Otherwise than Being*, 8.

64. Szendy, *Musica Practica*, 27.

65. Among the many threads I will not be able to develop is the transformative nature of what I otherwise refer to as a "rapport with self." But Szendy does delve into the "plastic" nature of such relations insofar as they occur within very distinct realms and, indeed, selves. *Plasticity* is a recurring word throughout Szendy's work; it is also the title of a conference (now a book) in which he participated and where he demonstrates the inventiveness of multiple, plastic selves (see Catherine Malabou, ed., *Plasticité* [Paris: Léo Scheer, 2000]; see also Catherine Malabou's own work on plasticity, change, transformation, and, indeed, conversion, most recently, *Le change Heidegger: Du fantastique en philosophie* [Paris: Léo Scheer, 2004]).

66. Michel Foucault, *The Hermeneutics of the Subject: Lectures at the Collège de France 1981–1982*, ed. Frédéric Gros, trans. Graham Burchell (New York: Picador, 2005), 207; Foucault recalls that, in the notion of conversion as deployed in the context of the care of the self, "one is not in fact dealing with a

rigorous, 'constructed' notion of conversion. It is much more a kind of practical schema, which although it is rigorously constructed, did not produce something like the 'concept' or notion of conversion" (207–8). As Meillassoux puts it, "this capacity-to-be-other cannot be conceived as a correlate of our thinking, precisely because it harbors the possibility of our own non-being" (Meillassoux, *After Finitude*, 57). With Szendy, we are attending to the possibility of generalizing such "practical schema."

67. Derrida, "Signature Event Context," 10.

68. Szendy, *Prophecies*, 47.

69. Pierre Hadot, *Philosophy as a Way of Life,* ed. and introd. Arnold I. Davidson, trans. Michael Chase (Oxford: Blackwell, 1995), 207.

70. Ibid., quoting Seneca.

71. Daniel Heller-Roazen beautifully shows that Seneca examined distinct kinds of selves, even animal selves, and most particularly "a movement, to be continually achieved anew throughout all animal life. It is a matter of the attention shown to the self by itself, to whose cultivation Seneca's Stoic colleagues Epictetus and Marcus Aurelius would most famously also turn in their explorations of the 'care of the self.' . . . Seneca, for his part, does not hesitate to invoke the practice in a letter devoted to the relation of every animal, rational and irrational, to itself" (Heller-Roazen, *The Inner Touch: Archaeology of a Sensation* [New York: Zone Books, 2007], 113).

72. Hadot, *Philosophy*, 207, quoting Seneca.

73. Ibid., 208.

74. Ibid.

75. Ibid.

76. Ibid., 211.

77. Ibid., 210–11. Cf. how for Foucault, or at least one of his interpreters, writing holds the promise of functioning quite precisely as a practice of freedom (even of *absolution*), as well as its opposite, of course: "Rhetoric makes individuals unfree by inscribing in them the self-relation they are already living—it subjects them to a particular interpretation of the human being" (Edward F. McGushin, *Foucault's* Askēsis: *An Introduction to the Philosophical Life* [Evanston, Ill.: Northwestern University Press, 2007], 29).

78. Hadot, *Philosophy*, 211.

79. Ibid.; emphasis added.

80. Ibid., 101; quoting Plotinus.

81. Marcel Mauss, "Techniques of the Body," trans. Ben Brewster, *Economy and Society* 2, no. 1 (February 1973): 70–88.

82. "The philosophers also forgot that speaking is a technique of the body," writes Kittler (*Discourse Networks*, 112). For a compelling demonstration of the pertinence of a Maussian approach as a complement to Foucault's lexicon,

see Charles Hirschkind (who incidentally shares many of Szendy's concerns—including Benjamin) on what he calls "the flesh of the ear," an "ethics of listening," and "listening as performance" (Hirschkind, *The Ethical Soundscape: Cassette Sermons and Islamic Counterpublics* [New York: Columbia University Press, 2006], 25, 67, 84); see also Talal Asad, *Formations of the Secular: Christianity, Islam, Modernity* (Stanford: Stanford University Press, 2003).

83. Up to this point, all quotations in this paragraph are from Foucault, *Hermeneutics of the Subject*, 15.

84. Hadot, *Philosophy*, 91.

85. Ibid., 81.

86. Talal Asad, *Genealogies of Religion: Discipline and Reasons of Power in Christianity and Islam* (Baltimore: Johns Hopkins University Press, 1993), 47.

87. Commenting on Foucault's use of the term, McGushin acknowledges that "we usually think of spirituality in terms of rituals of purification, renunciation of everyday concerns, denial of the body, overcoming desires, refuting the senses, and so on" (McGushin, *Foucault's Askēsis*, 80). McGushin tries to suggest that this is not the proper way to understand Foucault's "spirituality," but no account is provided of the pouring, as it were, of new wine into old skins (see 38–39). Recall that the "care of the self offers a possible counterpractice" to the biopolitical project "in the form of alternative techniques of self-fashioning," as McGushin rightly points out earlier (xx).

88. Hadot, *Philosophy*, 84, citing Philo Judaeus.

89. Ibid., 86.

90. According to the *Oxford English Dictionary*, an autophon is "a musical instrument that produces sound through the vibration of its constituent material." Accordingly, "autophony," the title of this section, is the "observation by a practitioner of the peculiarities of resonance of his own voice, when he places his head close to the chest of a patient, and speaks loudly." Szendy deploys the word in *Membres fantômes*, e.g., 37, 49, 83. In a longer section of the same book, entitled "Organologiques (2): L'autophonie," Szendy writes of "these figures that must be pushed aside by a respectable and reasonable organology as if they were jokes or bad dreams, fictitious monsters or chimera" (86).

91. Szendy, *Listen*, 71.

92. Ibid. Cf. how Kittler asserts that "the discourse network of 1900 could not build on the three functions of production, distribution, and consumption" (Kittler, *Discourse Networks*, 186).

93. Szendy, *Listen*, 72.

94. Ibid., 81.

95. Ibid., 82; emphasis added.

96. Walter Benjamin, "The Paris of the Second Empire," in *The Writer of Modern Life*, 86.

97. Szendy, *Listen*, 82.

98. Ibid.

99. Ibid., 81.

100. "Data-storage machines are much too accurate to make the classical distinction between intention and citation, independent thought and the mere repetition of something already said. They register discursive events without regard for so-called persons" (Kittler, *Discourse Networks*, 300).

101. Szendy, *Listen*, 87.

102. Ibid., 91.

103. Ibid., 97.

104. Ibid., 137.

105. In *Surécoute*, Szendy speaks of "the listening *of* music [*l'écoute* de *la musique*]," underscoring the double genitive, while insisting that it is the subjective genitive that interests him: "before being heard by someone, before becoming the object of an empirical listening, music would be listening (to itself) [*la musique (s')écouterait elle-même*], according to *its own* distant hearing, according to a tele-listening that would be its *own*" (Szendy, *Surécoute*, 57).

106. Szendy, *Listen*, 106.

107. Ibid., 113–14.

108. Ibid., 114.

109. Ibid., 117.

110. Ibid., 127.

111. Ibid., 139.

112. Ibid., 142.

113. Szendy, *Membres fantômes*, 142.

114. Ibid., 127–28.

115. For a compelling critical discussion of personification, see Bracken, *Magical Criticism*, 72ff., and Johnson, *Persons and Things*; for the proliferating (and current) insistence of an exclusively human "self," see: Taylor, *Sources of the Self*; Richard Sorabji, *Self: Ancient and Modern Insights about Individuality, Life, and Death* (Chicago: University of Chicago Press, 2006); as well as Jean Bethke Elshtain, *Sovereignty: God, State, and Self* (New York: Basic Books, 2008). "One of the most obvious assumptions we make," writes Barbara Johnson, "is that the human 'self' is a person, not a thing." And indeed, "nothing Descartes writes proves that the being whose existence he had demonstrated was human" (Johnson, *Persons and Things*, 47, 51). Szendy's generalized ipsology is obviously an attempt to take the measure of such statements.

116. Szendy, *Membres fantômes*, 87.

117. The Greek root or its derivatives cannot be equated with the notion of self that Szendy elaborates, of course (although an autophonic instrument is, in fact, called *idiophone* in French). Moreover, it exceeds the phenomenon

of idiocy and takes us into the greater realm of idiosyncrasy, idiom, idiolect, and those phenomena Szendy calls "idiotisms" (as well as "idiots in music"; 38–40). Much could be made of the structural echoes between the self and the stupid. Both terms bring us in the proximity of the infinite and of the absolute, as Avital Ronell has made strikingly clear: "Protected from any alterity, making to and of itself, enveloped by a narcissistic certitude that rhymes internally—being, in sum, without a care—stupidity may well approximate a plenitude. Replete in itself, immune to criticism, without resistance or the effort of negativity" (Ronell, *Stupidity* [Urbana: University of Illinois Press, 2002], 44). One wonders about the self, oneself, and other selves, and about the care (or lack thereof) of the self. From the telephone to the idiot and beyond (and the beyond), there would be much to gain in attending to the Benjaminian sensibilities—the beautiful and monstrous selves—of both Ronell and Szendy, something I can only allude to here.

118. Derrida, *Limited Inc*, 10.

119. Szendy, *Surécoute*, 148.

120. The motif—if one can call it that—of the double agent provides another thread, deserving much more attention than I am able to devote to it here, that parallels the structure of the mark (of the selves) that Szendy pursues and is pursued by in *Surécoute*. The logic of doubling to which it testifies can be extended to the entirety of his work, as I am trying to show: "tout semble se redoubler," writes Szendy, "everything seems to double itself" (*Surécoute*, 19). Taussig offers a proximate account when he suggests that "what enhances the mimetic faculty is *a protean self with multiple images (read 'souls') of itself* set in a natural environment whose animals, plants, and elements are spiritualized to the point that nature 'speaks back' to humans, every material entity paired with an occasionally visible spirit-double—a mimetic double!—of itself" (Taussig, *Mimesis and Alterity*, 97).

121. While this is not quite a new direction in Szendy's work, his attention is increasingly turning to the self of texts, to reading as a rapport to self of a text. This should be obvious to any reader of *Prophecies* and of the Preface to its English-language edition, but there is much more, and more to come.

122. Szendy, *Membres fantômes*, 141.

123. Ibid., 109, 123–25.

124. Ibid., 19.

125. Szendy, *Surécoute*, 17.

126. Szendy, *Tubes*, 26.

127. Jean-Luc Nancy, *The Inoperative Community*, trans. Peter Connor et al. (Minneapolis: University of Minnesota Press, 1991), 49; quoted in Szendy, *Tubes*, 26n1.

128. Szendy, *Tubes*, 26n1; on the haunting melody, with and beyond Theodor Reik's study by that title, see *Tubes*, 43–52.

129. Ibid., 77; Bracken also engages Nancy and his predecessors on myth, individuals such as Herbert Spencer, according to whom "'*mythos* is the *act of language* par excellence,' but an act in which 'being engenders itself *by figuring itself*'" (Bracken, *Magical Criticism*, 61, quoting Spencer). What for Nancy is "autofictioning" and "prosopopoeia" is, for Bracken, the paradoxical confinement of "barbarism" (or "animism") to the other, rather than to the self (62, 64).

130. Szendy, *Surécoute*, 73.

131. Nietzsche, *Thus Spoke Zarathustra*, 23; quoted in Szendy, *Membres fantômes*, 16.

132. Szendy, *Membres fantômes*, 17.

133. Ibid., 57.

134. Ibid., 60.

135. Ibid., 37, 97.

136. Szendy, *Membres fantômes*, 83, 90, 103, 131, 141, 142.

137. Jacques Derrida, *Monolingualism of the Other; or, The Prosthesis of Origin*, trans. Patrick Mensah (Stanford: Stanford University Press, 1998),14.

138. Jacques Derrida, *Rogues: Two Essays on Reason*, trans. Pascale-Anne Brault and Michael Naas (Stanford: Stanford University Press, 2005), 10–11.

139. Ibid., 11.

140. Meillassoux, *After Finitude*, 115–16; see also Jambet, *The Act of Being*, quoted above on the notion of 'world.'

141. R. E. Watters, "Melville's 'Isolatoes,'" *PMLA* 60, no. 4 (December 1945): 1138; quoting *Moby-Dick*, 27:121. Mary Douglas famously came to propose the term *isolates* to designate those she had described earlier at degree zero of the "grip and group" notion. These find themselves in areas "where populations are sparse and social relations infrequent, interrupted and irregular." There, "a person does not have the impression of inhabiting a man-dominated world. . . . He is controlled by objects not persons." For him "the cosmos is not anthropomorphic" (Douglas, *Natural Symbols: Explorations in Cosmology* [London: Routledge, 1996], 71). According to Douglas, though, "objects do not respond to personal modes of approach" and "there is no call for articulate forms of social intercourse with non-human beings" (ibid.; see also Mary Douglas and Steven Ney, *Missing Persons: A Critique of the Social Sciences* [Berkeley: University of California Press, 1998], 113ff.).

142. Szendy, *Prophecies*, "Isolation, The Bubble, and the Future of the Text," 79; just before, Szendy writes of "a congregation of atoms properly

*isolated"* (ibid.). In a proximate context, Branka Arsic refers to "celibatory machines." This is a machine, she explains, that "gives birth to a world, to be
sure, but because that world-writing remains absorbed into itself it refers only
to itself" (Arsic, *Passive Constitutions*, 125), adding later on that it is "one divided in itself remaining enclosed within itself and therefore neither one nor
double" (130).

143. Szendy, *Prophecies*, "Isolation, The Bubble, and the Future of the
Text," 81; the word *monadic*, as it appears here, is the only hint in Szendy's
work I have found of an engagement with Leibniz's *Monadologie*. It must
await further elaborations.

144. Gabriele Schwab attends to what she calls "subjects without selves" in
*Moby-Dick* (Schwab, *Subjects Without Selves: Transitional Texts in Modern Fiction* [Cambridge: Harvard University Press, 1994]; the phrase "meditative
transcendence of the self" is found on p.50). It should be obvious by now
that Szendy would be more accurately described as pursuing "selves without
subject."

145. Szendy, *Prophecies*, "Leviathan is the text," 44.

146. Szendy, *Prophecies*, "I," 7.

147. Derrida, *Speech and Phenomena*, 65. "Things appear and are discussed
as presences," writes Barbara Johnson, reminding us that there is a rapport
with presence and to nonpresence "in" things (Johnson, *Persons and Things*,
208); see also the next note.

148. Szendy, *Prophecies*, "Naming and Meteoromancy," 21; see also *Speech
and Phenomena*, where Derrida explains that "the presence of the perceived
present can appear as such only inasmuch as it is *continuously compounded*
with a nonpresence and nonperception, with primary memory and expectation
(retention and protention)" (64). This "ever renewed upsurge," which enables
as "it radically destroys any possibility of a simple self-identity," this "constituting flux" is indeed a storm, or a self (66).

149. Szendy, *Prophecies*, "Leviathan is the text," 8.

150. Ibid., "Before Sight, the Voice," 16.

151. Ibid., "Leviathan is the text," 47; "The Fire, the Bonds," 50; quoting
Meillassoux for the last time, this possibility is "the absolute whose reality is
thinkable as that of the in-itself as such [*l'en-soi*] in its indifference to thought;
an indifference which confers upon it the power to destroy me" (Meillassoux,
*After Finitude*, 57).

152. Szendy, *Prophecies*, "The Laws of Fishing and of Reading," 55.

153. Ibid., "In Detachment," 58.

154. Szendy, *Tubes*, 92.

155. Szendy, *Prophecies*, "Backfire," 78.